Ministry Marketing Made Easy

A Practical Guide to Marketing Your Church Message

Yvon Prehn

Abingdon Press
Nashville

Ministry Marketing Made Easy:
A Practical Guide to Marketing Your Church Message

Copyright © 2004 Yvon Prehn

This book is printed on acid-free, recycled paper.

Library of Congress Cataloging-in-Publication Data

Prehn, Yvon, 1959-
 Ministry marketing made easy: a practical guide to marketing your church
message / Yvon Prehn.
  p. cm.
 Includes bibliographical references.
 ISBN 0-687-05733-7 (alk. paper)
 1. Church marketing.   I. Title.

 BV652.23.P74 2004
 254—dc22   2004014342

04 05 06 07 08 09 10 11 12 13—10 9 8 7 6 5 4 3 2 1
MANUFACTURED IN THE UNITED STATES OF AMERICA

This book is dedicated to the people of RISO. You are the most extraordinary group of people I have ever had the joy of working with. Only heaven knows the churches you enrich and the lives you encourage by helping host my seminars. I cannot thank you enough for how hard you work to make it all possible. What a joy you've been to travel and work with—for that I dedicate this book to all of you.

Contents

Acknowledgements

This is an expanded dedication section where I get to name names. It's one of the perks of being an author. Unless you're Stephen King, there aren't many other perks to be had. Being an author is not an exciting, romantic vocation. It consists of days spent glued to the computer without breaks, gaining weight because you don't have time to work out, and eating lots of chocolates and coffee to keep motivated. My house becomes a pigsty, and when the book is finished I have to spend a month apologizing to friends, family, and business associates whose e-mails and phone calls I haven't answered while working frantically toward the deadline. Through it all, I looked forward to acknowledging publicly the extraordinary team of people who have shaped my life and ministry over the past eight years—the people of RISO. I'd like to acknowledge you in groups because I have come to know you based on these groups. (Some of you have shifted back and forth, so it won't be easy.)

I want to acknowledge the DSMs, Senior DSMs, BSMs and associated staff, the people I have worked with most directly. We have shared so many adventures as we've traveled all over the U.S. and Canada together, sometimes in very challenging situations. We've flown into every small town in Texas when the summer winds made little planes bounce like toys and we were terrified. We've driven and flown through blizzards, hurricanes, hailstorms, and windstorms. We've taken magical trips in the Maritimes and among the islands between Vancouver and Victoria. We've done seminars in the winter in New York City and then walked to see the Christmas tree, and in Fargo, N.D. where there wasn't a fancy Christmas tree, but there were almost 200 people with really warm hearts. We held a seminar at a camp on Puget Sound, and one on a river boat, even though I thought I was going to throwup any minute. We've done seminars in community centers, in small churches with grazing cows and cornfields outside, in wind- and rain-blown tents, in fancy and historic hotels, and in churches both extraordinary and humble.

You've taught me so much, like how to use airline and hotel points, and what kind of luggage lasts. You've gone far above the line of duty as you drove all night to get to a seminar when the airline wasn't flying, bought me lots of Cheetos and diet Coke on long drives down south between cities, and let me stop at the rest stops no matter how often I asked. You've done special things when we had time, like taking me to see the Longhorns in Texas, stopping in Hershey, Pa. to buy chocolates and lean out the windows and smell the chocolate fragrance that really does fill the air, and driving me past shipyards, universities, and local sites on the way to the airport. This was the fun stuff for me, but these things don't begin to touch the hours of work you put into reaching churches for my seminars. You visited strangers, spent hours on the phone, delivered information, and patiently answered questions. You were kind when people treated you with suspicion, and gentle when a church secretary asked for the hundredth time, "Who is this Yvon Prehn and how will that seminar help me?" No matter what, you worked to make it happen. Churches were equipped and encouraged, and lives were changed. To the people of RISO, I dedicate this book. I thank you, and pray the Lord will greatly reward you. In addition to the dedication, I want to acknowledge:

DSMs past and present: Bill Adams, Dave Ashcraft, Ben Bathen, Don Braswell, Kate Brothers, Dennis Burger, Rob Clark, Dave Collyer, Ray Cottiers, John Clayton, Andre D'Urbano, Howard Glick, Patrick Kierre, Lanny Meek, Bill Michalec, Paul Myers, Walt Perkins, Holly Recalde, Dennis Smith, Jeff Stanley, Rich Walker, Kevin Wright, Shea Vara-Heck. BSMs and Special Staff, past and present: Jack Rubeck, Darryl Clinton, Larry Jennings, Gary Plinario, Kelli Moss, Rod Christian, Kurt Gilbert, Keith Hinson, David St. Leger, Dan Rafferty, Jeff Bianca, Wayne Starkey, Bev Matushewski, Ellen Meehan, Gord Leah, Karl Kronenbery, Phil Caswell, Mark Thomas, Hal Ottersen, Ted Funsch, Sue Davis, Doug Blair, Alan Lefkowitz, Robert Evanko, Pam Stephan. In this section I also want to include special people who work with these folks in various ways and who have been a great part of the success of the seminars: David Murphy, Harold Zuckerman, Tony Teti, Don McQuaid, Gord Leah, Ed Morovec, and Kevin Thompson.

I also want to acknowledge the leadership of RISO and the people who work at RISO headquarters. Your vision equips the churches of the world with tools that make it possible for them to effectively share the gospel message. This is just one reflection of the greatness of your company. The integrity, professionalism, and kindness of the people of RISO start at the top, and I thank you for the privilege of working with you. The leadership and support people of RISO in the various parts of the country, past and present, (please forgive me if I have left out some headquarters people whom I haven't been in touch with personally) I want to acknowledge and thank are: Dan Weil, Todd Deluca, Rick Mytnik, Mike Maki, Richie Grassis, Maurice Yenni, Jack Ford, Kevin Hunter, Robin Mazer, Bernie Rainford, Kathleen Ryan, Michele Pszenny, Anne Barrett, Alex Olshan, Louise Greto, Suzanne Farley, Karen Schmuch, Joanne Perrault, Kristen Williams, Verne Westgate, Beth Allen, Susan Daurio, and in a category all his own, Bill McKenna.

And finally, all the incredible dealers and dedicated RISO and church reps—your service to the churches and kindness to me has been extraordinary. Without your help, many church bulletins would never have been printed and many lives would not have been blessed. Thank you.

Introduction

Why is marketing needed in the church today?

Because many people outside the church have our story wrong. The ending of the gospel story for believers in Jesus is truly to live happily ever after. There will be trials on the journey, but the trials will end. Heaven is a certainty. All wrongs will be righted, all hurts healed. Rewards will be given for every kind and brave deed. All of heaven will applaud.

"And here's the thing. The Gospel is a fairy story that's true. There really is a curse. There really is a dragon. But the amazing thing is: God sent His son . . . And those who trust Him will live happily ever after." [1]
—Dr. Richard Mouw, president of Fuller Seminary

But not everyone has heard the true story.

Without that hearing, people believe distorted stories. The God of love and compassion is portrayed as a despot arbitrarily inflicting pain on people the same way a small boy may torture a bug. Other false reports assert God has lost interest and walked away, leaving us to fight and squabble without hope of justice or resolution. In the saddest tale of all some people don't believe their lives are part of any story, but simply a blot of sadness, scribbled without hope and shortly erased.

Ministry Marketing is all about telling the true story.

The Foundation for Ministry Marketing Made Easy

To tell the gospel story with Ministry Marketing involves more than finding the latest and greatest innovation in either technology or technique. We cannot rely on technology or technique to tell our story, "wow" the world, and have it flock to our churches. To understand the state we are in regarding marketing in the church and how to change it, we've first got to look inside ourselves.

> *For out of the overflow of the heart the mouth speaks.*
> —Matthew 12:34, NIV
>
> *For as he thinketh in his heart, so is he.*
> —Proverbs 23:7, KJV

That's where this section starts. Before learning how to do easy Ministry Marketing, we must understand why we are in the present situation. This section begins by analyzing where we are in telling our story, and why we tell it the way we do.

Various Ministry Marketing misconceptions are also presented and solutions provided. These misconceptions keep many churches from intentionally using marketing as an outreach tool.

Next, this section looks at the unspoken purposes that drive Marketing Ministry in many churches, and it proposes three intentional Ministry Marketing purposes that will give your church the ability to run and complete the race needed for Ministry Marketing success. Section One also identifies three assumptions by which churches unthinkingly operate. These assumptions kill opportunities for successful Ministry Marketing.

Finally, this section identifies the characteristics of church Ministry Marketing audiences.

Don't skip this first section. We live out the daily tasks of our days from the convictions of our hearts. We won't do something as challenging as sustained Ministry Marketing if we aren't deeply convinced of its importance. I trust that this section will give you the background and insights needed to create a foundation of conviction and a purpose that will make your Ministry Marketing activities easy and effective.

CHAPTER 1:

The Status of Our Story

Why the confusion? After all:

We have the greatest message. Our story contains the wonderful message that Jesus came into our world in human form, went to the cross to pay the penalty for our sins, rose from the dead, and offers forgiveness and eternal life for all who trust Him as Savior. Not only do Christians believe this message by faith, but the gospel story also can be verified historically and scientifically. It can answer satisfactorily the questions of any honest skeptic.[3]

We have powerful tools. Every person working on a computer in today's church has a more powerful system than NASA had when it put a man on the moon. We have software that allows churches to create printed materials that entire nations could not produce in the past. Some churches have multi-media systems able to instruct and entertain thousands of people. With digital duplication systems like the RISO, we have a printing press that Gutenberg would envy. The Internet allows us to reach the entire world, and we can touch shut-ins and countries closed to Christian missions.

> *One of the most frequently used phrases in Christian circles is "the gospel." Amazingly few adults know what this term means. It could either refer to its literal translation, "good news;" or to the perspective that salvation is available only through the sacrificial death and subsequent resurrection of Jesus Christ and a person's acceptance of Christ as their savior. Less than four out of ten adults (37%) knew this; 34% had other, inaccurate perceptions of the meaning of the term; three out of ten adults did not offer a guess. Even among born again Christians, only 60% correctly identified at least one meaning of this expression.[2]*
> —From Barna Research Online

We have well-thought-out church growth programs. If we need help learning how to tell our story, there are leaders and churches that provide a pattern for us. Rick Warren and Saddleback Church, Bill

Hybels and Willow Creek Church, Mike Slaughter and Ginghams-burg Church[4] are some of the pastors, churches, and programs I am most familiar with because of my background, but there are many more. In my seminars, I talk to brothers and sisters from every denomination and branch of the Christian church, including Roman Catholic, charismatic, Orthodox, ethnic, and emerging churches. Each one has programs to grow churches and to deepen the spiritual lives of members.

We have extraordinary people. I don't know anyone who works harder or cares more passionately about sharing the gospel story than people who work in the church. Though often underpaid and overworked, people in the church communicate with passion and excitement because they know what they do makes life more bearable on earth and alters the destinies of souls for eternity.

The big question

Why, then, isn't the whole world a Christian world?

We have the greatest message, the most powerful tools, well-conceived church growth programs, and extraordinary people working on them. Why are Christians statistically and culturally losing the hearts and minds of the people of our world? Why is it that so few people know the true story of Jesus and the Christian faith? I believe our problem isn't our message, tools, programs, or people.

My conclusion: Our problem is that we aren't marketing or communicating our message very well.

The medium isn't the message

Some people have called Marshall McLuhan the "high priest of popculture."[5] However, with all due respect, I believe that McLuhan's well-known saying, "the medium is the message," has led thousands of communicators astray, especially in the church. This statement and current technological challenges have caused many communicators to focus foremost on the tools they use to create their messages, rather than the content of the message itself. I have observed in the last several years this focus on mastering the new tools of technology has caused many churches to become lax about communicating the church's message clearly.

In stating the "medium is the message," McLuhan helped us to see that the media used to present a message becomes part of the message itself. Things go slightly off track in practice, however, when McLuhan's phrase is subtly turned into, "The medium makes the message successful."

"We did it with desktop publishing!" "We have a new projection system in the church!" "We now have a web site!" and similar affirmations can be heard when a church finally figures out how to use some new technology. This subtle (and often unspoken or misanalysed) shift assumes that if we master the marketing communication tools, including desktop publishing programs, multimedia and projection software, and web sites, then our message will be successfully communicated. Mastering the medium has become the focus of our energies.

The world is not impressed.

Our use of new media is not what sets the Church apart

It's the content of our message that is the unique story for the world, not the medium used to present it. We've garbled the story—not just the grand theme of salvation but also the details of our individual stories: the times, places, and specifics that make the story tangible. When we lose these details, we lose the link that people need to connect to the great story. The practical result of losing this link by emphasizing the technology and not the details is that people don't show up for programs and ministries sponsored by the church. For example:

• Before the church service, an awesome youth-themed, Power-Point® background is on the screen. It announces an upcoming Saturday night lock-in, complete with the latest popular music to accompany the youthful and relevant, animated graphics. But there isn't a bulletin insert provided or a postcard sent out during the week that gives parents and teenagers the time, location, and how much money is needed for the lock-in. Few youth show up.

17

The following Sunday the disappointed youth director talks to dozens of kids who respond, "I didn't know it was this weekend."

Suggested solution: *A simple printed reminder, either a postcard, flyer, or bulletin insert that could have been posted on the refrigerator would have drastically changed the attendance at the lock-in.*

• A church newsletter has the awesome graphics, abundance of white space, and typography choices that could win awards, but the writing is boring and judgmental. The topics would interest the author's seminary professors. The church leadership believes that to discuss "need-centered" topics would be to dilute the message. They also feel it is a waste of space to use the newsletter for activity announcements. At the same time they are frustrated because few people pick up the newsletter from the tables in the church lobby. "Nobody cares about the church today," the church leaders complain.

Suggested solution: *People care about what meets their needs. If the newsletter spoke to genuine needs and contained useful activity information, people would read it. Generous white space, beautiful type and guilt-inducing writing are not terribly high on anyone's felt-need list.*

• A church proclaims, "PEOPLE MATTER TO US!" with professionally produced banners hung on the outside of the building. But once inside, the church doesn't provide maps or directions to the nursery or the bathrooms, and there is no handicapped access to the adult classes. The church bulletin contains no order of service, because it is assumed that everyone knows what happens during the church service. Singing (with everyone standing) goes on for the first forty-five minutes. Few visitors return a second week.

Suggested solution: *A simple order of service that explains what is happening and gives people permission to sit down if they want to during the singing (of songs they don't know) says people matter much more convincingly than a flashy banner does.*

The message is the message

Everything—the medium used to share the message, the tools used to create it, the money spent, how it looks—has a place, but the means should not be the primary concern. The message is the message. What is in our hearts, how we care about people, and how clearly and lovingly we work to proclaim the gospel message will be communicated no matter what tools we use to physically produce our message or how much money it costs. Realizing that the message is the message, the content matters, and the story is the essential thing you must communicate, is what makes Ministry Marketing easy. You do not need to take complex surveys or work up elaborate marketing charts, graphs, and plans. You do not need a fifty-thousand-dollar projection system, a killer web site, or thousands of dollars to spend on direct mail marketing campaigns. These things may be nice, but they are not essential to easy and successful Ministry Marketing.

You simply need to tell the gospel story and the stories of your church clearly, completely, and frequently. That's what easy Ministry Marketing is all about, and that's what this book will help you do.

Before I tell you how to make steady Ministry Marketing success happen, I want to share my background with you. I want you to understand why I assert the things I do with such confidence. This is not required reading and may be skipped if you want to go straight to the theory and how-to sections of the book.

My story and the source of the stories shared in this book

My confidence in and excitement about sharing these marketing examples and suggestions comes from two sources—my story and the stories of the tens of thousands of people I have had the joy to interact with in my seminars on church communications and marketing.

At present, my story during many weeks of the year starts at around 4:30 a.m. on Monday morning. Half asleep I shower, dress, and go back to sleep for two hours during a car ride to Los Angeles

International Airport. Once there, most weeks I catch an early flight on United Airlines to Chicago. I refer to it as my work commute.

During the four-hour flight I usually try to write while juggling lots of coffee and fighting off Dramamine sleepiness. From Chicago's O'Hare airport, after grabbing a green protein drink from The Grove (a great juice and snack shop in all three United terminals at O'Hare), I connect to wherever I'm going to be teaching seminars on Christian communication and marketing what week. It might be Philadelphia, Reading, Harrisburg, Baltimore, or Nashville, Memphis, Little Rock, or Grand Rapids, Lansing, Travers City, as was the case during three weeks in 2003. I do between sixty to eighty seminars a year all over the U.S. and Canada. I've been doing this full-time for the last eight years. Prior to that I led similar seminars, though less frequently, for over twenty years.

My seminars (current information and schedules may be found on my web site at www.cyberservants.org or www.ministrycom.com) are held in hotels, conference centers, and large churches. Attendance ranges from twenty-something to almost 200. The attendees come from every Christian denomination and include pastors, church secretaries, and volunteers—anyone who is interested in learning how to better communicate and market the Christian story. Many participants attend because communication in their local churches isn't going very well.

At the end of the day participants leave excited, energized, and ready to market their message in ways both more powerful and simple than they ever imagined.

I go back to some of the same places year after year. The reports of Ministry Marketing and communication success and the joy of lives changed as a result of changes made in publications are what keep me getting on those airplanes. (However, I still believe flying is one of the most unnatural and scary activities a human being can do.)

The background that qualified me to teach seminars began when my father retired from the Army to Colorado Springs. Colorado Springs was a wonderful place to grow up for someone who wanted to be a writer and a teacher for Jesus. It is the headquarters of approximately 100 Christian organizations. On the teaching side of my life, I taught kindergarteners in Sunday School when I was in third grade, the fourth-graders when I was in sixth grade, and I took on the high school youth group when I was sixteen. I continued youth work for about twenty years and I've taught adult Sunday School classes off and on ever since.

On the writing and publication production side of my life, I have created my own materials for teaching since grade school. It's a lot easier to create printed teaching materials now. I've often said that no one can honestly appreciate desktop publishing unless he or she remembers the days of how hard it was to make a straight line using that press-on tape we used. My first memory of producing Sunday School handouts in grade school involved blue trays of gel (my publication production history does go back a bit). The mimeograph machine was a wonder to work with when I got old enough to be trusted with it. Cut and paste and press-on letters were great fun when I worked in high-school ministry. When I got a correcting typewriter in graduate school, I didn't think technology could ever get any better. When I graduated from high school I was told never to have anything to do with computers because my mind just wasn't wired that way. This advice was fine with me.

Though my first article was nationally published when I was sixteen, and I subsequently had been writing Christian books and articles for years, there were two things I'd never really learned to do very well: typing and spelling. These weaknesses made editors crazy. When I heard that something called a "spell-checker" had been invented I was motivated to learn the computer. The Kaypro was one of the first portable computers and it was my first computer. I say "portable" but it was about the size of the carry-on suitcase I fly with these days. I remember lugging it to one writer's conference in Wheaton, Ill., thinking I was *tres* cool. I wasn't, but I did write a book or two and quite a few articles with that machine.

I then went to work as senior editor at Compassion Intl., where we worked with mainframes and dumb terminals. A job as senior editor at Young Life International followed. At Young Life we had our own stand-alone PCs. We also had a complete in-house print shop, layout artists, and typesetting. There I learned all about traditional printing, production, and publication design.

I was at Young Life when desktop publishing was invented. When I first saw this technology used I said, "This is going to change everything we do in Christian communications," and it has. It took us months to produce publications at Young Life using traditional typesetting, layout, and printing. One person with a computer and a laser printer could now do the same tasks in a matter of hours. It was a new world.

Shortly after that, unfortunately or fortunately in the sovereign plan of God, Young Life shut down in-house print operation and I was out on my own, teaching churches and Christian ministries how to do marketing and communications. When I was in Colorado Springs I taught classes and consulted with numerous Christian organization in the area, including: Greater Europe Mission, AFMIN, Eastern European Bible Mission, Youth with a Mission, Navigators, Focus on the Family, Single Ministry Resources, Teen Challenge, International Students, The Salvation Army, Christian Management Association, Christian Camping Intl., Evangelical Press Association, Christian Missionary Alliance, Prison Fellowship and many other nonprofit and church-related organizations. I also started a communication ministry and taught people how to use this new technology in lots of churches in Colorado Springs and at national conferences.

In 1994 I married my wonderful husband, Paul, and we moved to Ventura, Ca. where he worked as Pastor of Single Adults. At that time I was writing about desktop publishing and communications for a number of Christian publications, and I had completed some books on that topic. I was (and still am) the desktop publishing columnist for *Christian Computing Magazine.*[6] I was also teaching seminars on Christian communication and marketing at national seminars all over the U.S.

My seminar teaching intensified when the RISO Corporation called and asked if they could sponsor some of my seminars. The RISO Corporation is the company that produces the RISO Digital Duplicator. RISO is a Japanese company with the intentional focus in public relations to serve their potential customers. RISO sponsors seminars that may be of interest to potential customers and if people are interested, they may look at RISO's equipment during breaks. When RISO contacted me to see if they could sponsor some of my seminars my response was, "Well, here's the deal: I do an aggressively Christian seminar. I open with prayer. I quote the Bible and talk about Jesus all day long and I'm not changing a thing. Are you still interested?" They were, and the last eight years have been the most wonderful working experience of my life.

Because of my ongoing experience with RISO, I feel I've been given unique insights into where the church in North America stands in communications and marketing today. In my seminars during the last eight years, I estimate that I've interacted with more than 60,000 people, including church office workers, pastors, business administrators, and communication-producing volunteers from thousands of churches.

People come to my seminars from denominations of every size and economic situation imaginable. I've talked to many participants during breaks and lunch. I've listened to their stories. I've cried with some and have been angry with others over the petty insults they receive from church members who believe their mission in life is to point out every typo made by the church secretary. I've been frustrated by the challenging working conditions that many church workers must endure. I've celebrated with them when lives are changed because a Ministry Marketing project was successful.

It is from their stories and from looking at their publications that I have learned so much that I believe will be helpful to you.

One more part of my story shapes what I am sharing. Often, when Thursday night comes and the last seminar is over, I dash back to the airport to catch a connecting flight to Chicago, then endure the five-hour plane trip home. (It takes longer going west; you fly against the trade winds.) During that time I usually do one of two things. First, I look over the samples of church publications people have given me at the seminar. I see patterns, make notes, and get ideas. I've learned from these samples that for all of our surface differences, church publications are remarkably similar—so many people struggle with the same communication and marketing challenges—and I work on ways to help solve some of the problems. I also get great ideas, many of which I will share in this book. (You will find other good ideas on my web site, www.cyberservants.com or www.ministrycom.com.)

Second, I use the time to work on communication and marketing materials for my own church. My husband's story is that of a pastor. For the last number of years he has been a bi-vocational pastor who has worked primarily in the areas of single adult ministry, Christian education, and small groups. Paul is a big, 6 ' 3 ", 250-pound, teddy bear of a man who loves Jesus and wants the world to get to know Jesus. One of our greatest joys is to team teach Sunday School classes. On the flight home, I often work on the lesson, the handouts, the postcards or verse cards, the class newsletters, and lots of the projects I'll talk about in more detail later.

This last part of my life is one of the most important for you to know because I would never presume to tell you, the people who work in the church, how to do Ministry Marketing publications if I was not continuously working on these projects and publications myself. Marketing from inside the church is a unique experience, and unless you're living it, no statistical study in the world can teach you about it. I always chuckle at books written by "experts" who do a study, tabulate the results, and then give some profound advice, such as, "A demographically suitable mailing campaign targeted to your economically appropriate audience will generate significant response."

Yeah, right. And who will create the postcards, put the labels on them, and pay for the postage? The "experts" never seem to address those minor details and many others like them. I do the work I tell you to do, and I won't share or recommend anything to you that I am not either doing or would be willing to do at my church. (By the way, I have a great postcard mailing solution that answers the situation above, later in the book.)

I could share many more stories that have made up my story of experiences in marketing and communication: my work as a religion writer for the *Colorado Springs Sun* newspaper, what I've learned from some of the great editors I've worked with, the many communications consulting projects I've done with churches and international organizations, the publications I've designed, but enough space has been used on my story. Now let me help you tell yours.

How this book is organized

The book has four sections, plus a lengthy Annotated Resource Section in the back.

Section One is the Foundation for Ministry Marketing Made Easy. Here, we will define what Ministry Marketing is, identify unworthy purposes people have for doing Ministry Marketing, and replace them with worthy purposes. We will also emphasize three killer Ministry Marketing assumptions, and discuss the characteristics of Ministry Marketing audiences today.

Section Two discusses the Characteristics of Easy Ministry Marketing. I could have included many characteristics, but the ones we discuss here describe Ministry Marketing as people-centered, precise, pop-culture savvy, and playful.

Section Three gives practical production advice for Key Ministry Marketing Publications, including invitation cards, postcards, church bulletins, church bulletin inserts, and niche newsletters.

Section Four outlines Strategic Implementation of Easy Ministry Marketing. These strategies are persistent, planned, programmed, publicity pro-active, pervasive, partnering, properly equipped, and prayer saturated.

Recommended books, products, materials, web sites, and resources

To do successful and easy Ministry Marketing, you need many resources. From my experience and from the experience of thousands of folks I have met in my seminars, I've collected many resources to recommend. Sometimes I merely mention the resource, and sometimes I make suggestions with great enthusiasm. Whatever the level of recommendation, please be aware that neither my ministry nor I receive income from any product, software, person, book, or anything recommend here or in the resource section. In addition, my ministry takes no advertising. It never has and it never will. I recommend what I like and I'll plainly express my opinion, if asked, if I don't like something. I sell some of my own stuff on my web site, but I don't talk about it here; you will have to find it if you are interested.

Please let me know if I've missed great tools, software, and resources that you'd recommend. Many of my recommendations come from people in my seminars. My e-mail is yvonprehn@aol.com. I can't promise to personally answer every e-mail, but I will answer all I can and guarantee I will read them all.

The book has many stories

In the stories shared all of the names and some of the details have been changed, and some stories have been combined, but each story is based on true situations that either I have observed or that participants in my seminars have shared with me. For all of you in my seminars who shared your stories verbally, on written bits of paper, or in emails, you helped to write this book, and I thank you.

CHAPTER 2:

Marketing Misconceptions Defined and Defused

This chapter contains an overview of basic Ministry Marketing definitions. It also addresses frequent marketing misconceptions and is intended to put your heart and mind at ease if you have spiritual questions and concerns about marketing. You will find this chapter helpful if you are asking these questions:

"Wait just a minute! What does marketing have to do with ministry? Marketing is worldly; ministry is spiritual."

"Ministry and marketing—can the two go together? Is it really a skill we can learn or an oxymoron created to sell a book?"

These are good questions and valid concerns.

> *Nonprofit organizations are involved in marketing whether or not they are conscious of it. They are involved in various markets and use certain operating principles in dealing with each market. These operating principles define their marketing. The issue is not one of whether or not nonprofit organizations should get involved in marketing, but rather how thoughtful they should be at it.*[7]
> —Phillip Kotler[3], Marketing for NonProfit Organizations

Marketing defined

First, let's look at Webster's definitions of the terms "ministry" and "marketing." Then read my modified definitions for the purposes of this book.

Webster's definitions:

ministry: the act of serving

marketing: the total of activities involved in the moving of goods from the producer to the consumer

My definition of Ministry Marketing

Combining the two definitions above and adapting them for the church results in this working definition:

> *Ministry Marketing: a servant ministry that consists of the sum of activities (every action and act of communication that makes up our story), involved in moving the good of salvation (from the God who produced it by the death and resurrection of Jesus) toward helping the intended consumer—a lost humanity—to accept that salvation."*

Or, said another way:

> *Ministry Marketing: everything we do in communications and actions as servants of Jesus to share His story and to invite people to join us in the eternal adventure of living it.*

One of the most important elements in this definition is the word *everything*. Ministry Marketing involves everything we do, including all communications, publications, media, and public actions of your church. You cannot create any publication, communication, or media in your church and not have it affect your marketing in either a positive or negative way.

Misconceptions about Ministry Marketing

Even with a good definition, many church people have four misconceptions about marketing. Let's define and address these misconceptions. The rebuttals to these misconceptions should remove any objections to instituting a more intentional marketing program in your church.

Marketing Misconception #1: Marketing's primary purpose is to draw attention to itself.

Marketing Misconception #2: Marketing is somehow unspiritual. At best it is a worldly tool that is used to manipulate people into making decisions that they would not otherwise make.

Marketing Misconception #3: Marketing only involves the communications created on paper or for the web.

Marketing Misconception #4: The task of marketing is a job for professionals only. It involves lots of time, money, expensive research, statistics, demographics, tools, and techniques beyond the resources of most churches and ministries.

Marketing Misconception #1: Marketing's primary purpose is to draw attention to itself

To address this valid concern, it is important to emphasize the adjective *ministry* to describe the kind of marketing we do in the church. Again, to minister means to serve. Church marketing is first, last, and always a servant ministry. It does not exist to draw attention to itself or to the people who produce the publications.

Our goal is not for people to say, "Wow, what a visually beautiful newsletter!" Our goal is not to win design awards or to impress people with cool typeface selection. Success in Ministry Marketing is measured differently than success in secular marketing. Success in Ministry Marketing is measured in lives changed, not in compliments heard or awards won. The measure of success for Ministry Marketing is the people who come to know Jesus as Savior and grow to maturity in their Christian lives. When it does this well, Ministry Marketing is a somewhat invisible ministry in the church.

You don't remember marketing if it is done well. Instead, you celebrate the results as the church grows, more people attend events, and the ministry prospers. While the pastor may be congratulated for his or her great talk, the trainer thanked for the great workshop, the evangelist praised for the revival, few notice or thank the people who worked hard to do the publicity and marketing for these events.

Check your motivation for doing Ministry Marketing

This reality reveals an important ministry caution: Don't go into Ministry Marketing and communications if you need public praise and thanks to keep going—you won't get it. If you work in church communications and marketing, the only time that you will be publicly acknowledged for your work is when you make a typo that makes somebody really angry. Then people will know who you are. Then you will be publicly recognized.

Marcie, a new church secretary, experienced this situation when she mistakenly published the wrong date for an upcoming event in her church. A gentleman in the church had not been terribly enthusiastic about some of the changes she'd made to the bulletin in recent weeks and he thought that her publication style was too youthful and modern. His disgruntlement had even led him to complain about the situation to the pastor. On the Sunday when the mistake appeared, he found it and yelled from his pew during the announcement time, "Pastor, tell people the correct date for the church anniversary picnic. Our new church secretary Marcie messed it all up."

Marcie slumped in her pew and wanted to die. She was ready to quit her job.

When Marcie shared her story with me, I understood why she felt the way she did. That sort of treatment is unkind and uncalled-for, but sadly is a common experience for those who work in church communication and marketing. In an attempt to encourage Marcie, I remind her that being involved in Ministry Marketing is a bit like being a Levite in the Old Testament times: The Lord is your only reward. In the Old Testament, the Levites couldn't own any land (Deut. 14:29). All the other tribes could, but not them. Like the Levites, the Lord is the only one who rewards you for much of the Ministry Marketing work you will do.

I also reminded Marcie that, though she might be the brunt of criticism and unappreciated work today, helping people come to know Jesus, even behind the scenes, is truly the way to become a star. Recall Daniel 12:3: "Those who are wise will shine like the brightness of the heavens, and those who lead many to righteousness, like the stars for ever and ever." (NIV)

Marcie was encouraged. It helps to have an eternal perspective on the value of Ministry Marketing and to focus on what will bring about eternal rewards.

In order to correct the first Ministry Marketing misconception, remember that Ministry Marketing isn't about drawing attention to itself, it's about bringing people to Jesus. Others may not recognize you for your work now, and they may even criticize you. But it won't always be that way. To encourage yourself in your work, put a little note above your desk that says, "Someday I'll be a star!"

Marketing misconception #2: Marketing is not spiritual

It's important to address this misconception because we certainly don't want to do anything that displeases the Lord. In voicing this fear, many people relate the story of Jesus chasing the money changers out of the temple (Matt. 21:12-13). People are afraid that anything that is even remotely connected to commerce should not be conducted in the church.

To address the concern, we need to remember that in the story about Jesus cleansing the Temple the characters who sold livestock and exchanged currency had nothing to do with marketing the gospel message. They were just selling their stuff. Ministry Marketing wasn't the issue in that situation. There are, however, valid examples of Ministry Marketing in scripture, as well as solid examples in today's church.

Biblical Ministry Marketing Example #1: The Apostle Paul

The Apostle Paul was one of the greatest marketers of all time. As Paul traveled, he usually went directly to the synagogue to speak. In this setting, he already knew his market well. However, Acts 17 describes his visit to Athens. Here it was different and in Athens, Paul engaged in some careful market research before he shared his messaged. Look closely: Here is a man who went around the city carefully studying the pagan idols. This was not easy for him to do. Paul was raised with "Thou shalt have no other gods before me," and "Thou shalt not make any graven image." Despite his background, Paul carefully studied what was personally repulsive to him because what he studied was important to the people he wanted to reach with the gospel message. Paul even took the time to memorize some of their poetry. When it came time for him to speak, instead of pronouncing curses on the worship of idols, Paul said, "I see that in every way you are very religious. For as I walked around and looked carefully at your objects of worship, I even found an altar with this inscription: TO AN UNKNOWN GOD. Now what you worship as something unknown I am going to proclaim to you." (Acts 17:22, 23, NIV).

This is Ministry Marketing in action—studying what is important to the audience you are trying to reach and then using that as a bridge to the gospel message. (For modern-day examples of how to build similar bridges, look at Chapter 7: Ministry Marketing Is Pop Culture Savvy.)

Ministry Marketing Example #2: Jesus

When Jesus began sharing his message publicly, he didn't stay home in Nazareth and post a little sign outside the carpenter's shop that said, "Interested in eternal life? Knock on my door." He didn't stay in Nazareth and wait for people to come to him. Instead, he was in the public arena each day, sharing and marketing his message in a way that was appropriate to his day and audience.

Ministry Marketing Example #3: Joshua

One last example on the spiritual value of marketing comes from a devotion by Charles Spurgeon.[8] Spurgeon begins by retelling the story of the children of Israel's battle with the Amalek (Exodus 17). In the story, Joshua is down in the valley fighting and Moses is up on the mountain with his hands raised in prayer. So long as Moses holds up his arms, the Israelites win. However, as Moses tires and his arms drop, the army begins to loose. So Aaron and Hur help hold up Moses' arms and the battle is won.

Spurgeon comments that we often use this story as an example of the importance of prayer in our spiritual battles, and that is a good application of the Bible story. But we must never forget that while Moses is up on the mountain praying, Joshua is in the valley fighting bloody, hand-to-hand combat. In all that we do for the Lord, Spurgeon continues, we must always do two things: We must pray, because every victory is ultimately God's, and we must also fight.

Don't just pray without taking action

This story is incredibly important for you to remember as you do the work of Ministry Marketing. The story of Joshua illustrates a recurrent problem in thousands of churches. The steps that make up the problem often occur something like this:

1. The church staff plans and envisions great and glorious activities, church growth events, and outreach programs.

2. The staff prays about the plans. They discuss. They hold committee meetings. They pray some more.

3. They recruit the people to put on a worthwhile ministry event. The event's details are perfectly in place. The program leaders practice and are ready to go.

4. The day of the event comes and almost nobody shows up.

Sound familiar? This is what happens far too often in churches. It is a modern-day example of Moses praying but no Joshua fighting. This book will help equip the Joshuas in your church to do their part.

The following story illustrates a real-life event that both underscores the reality of the story above and is a preview of a number of principles that will be discussed later in this book. It reveals problems in marketing church events and what happens when we pray and use expensive production media without simple, but intentional, marketing strategy and tools.

Real-life story about the limitations of prayers and good intentions

In this instance a church was experiencing great numerical growth. It had grown from 600 to more than 1,800 in attendance in three years. The Sunday service was spectacular, with seeker-sensitive music, drama, and powerful, need-centered preaching. Individuals were making decisions to become Christians every week and the church was growing in numbers. They were doing many things right.

Though grateful for the growth, the church staff was concerned because the growth was primarily reflected in Sunday morning service attendance. The leadership realized that people also needed to grow in

Christian maturity. The staff then decided to address this issue by initiating a men's ministry. The staff prayed about and planned for the kick-off event for the new men's ministry, and they advertised it for four weeks in the bulletin and newsletter, on PowerPoint®, and through lively announcements. The staff expected at least 100-200 men to show up. The night came for the event. The twelve men from the church staff and the planning leaders enthusiastically setup tables and chairs for 200, expecting a great response. Three men came. What went wrong? The staff did all the right things, spiritually. They followed a biblically sound ministry model, they planned and prayed, and then they prayed some more. They held more meetings and prayed more.

The marketing plan for the men's ministry

Though they did all the right things spiritually, the staff didn't do effective Ministry Marketing. This is how they marketed the event:

1. They advertised the study for four weeks in the newsletter and bulletin. Their belief concerning the effectiveness of these communication pieces was that the most important criteria for success was how the pieces looked. Therefore, the pieces were produced by a professional advertising agency in full-color on glossy paper.

2. The content of the announcement was the same in both the newsletter and the bulletin. It said, "Men's Bible study starting Sept. 8. All men of the church are encouraged to attend. Sign up in the church lobby."

3. They announced the event from the pulpit in the same way for three weeks, and used PowerPoint® each week to illustrate the announcement. The PowerPoint® presentation was attractive and well done.

What looked right and what went wrong

At first look it seems like a good way to market the program, so what went wrong? Here are some of the most obvious problems:

1. Though the event planners advertised the event a total of eight times in their printed material (a good number of

times), the announcement was virtually worthless because it didn't give the complete information details that would enable the men to attend the event. The planners did not tell the men the time the event was going to start or where it was going to be held.

It doesn't matter how beautiful the graphics are in a communication piece if essential details like these are left out. All of the details must be included every time and as a part of every announcement of an event if you want people to attend.

2. They made a number of incorrect Ministry Marketing assumptions: The staff assumed that men would find out the information regarding starting time and location, and would write it down and remember it when they went into the church lobby to sign up for the study. If you want to give any event the kiss of death and guarantee no response at all, tell people to "sign up in the church lobby." Nobody does, especially guys.

After church is over, does any man say to his wife (please forgive any implied sexism in this illustration), "Honey, would you please wait for me in the car while I find out where to go sign up for the men's Bible study?" It doesn't happen. I know my own husband's most pressing thought after church is (yes, you guessed it) food! Following the thought of food is football, basketball, or hockey, depending on the time of year. Most men I know, godly guys that they are, are similar.

Any time you require people to take a second step (call the church office for more information, sign up in the lobby, etc.) to find out essential details that they need to show up, you will drastically cut down attendance at your ministry event.

Summary of incorrect Ministry Marketing assumptions

• **The staff assumed that men would remember the details from the PowerPoint®** announcement presented every Sunday. Most men don't. PowerPoint® is great for song lyrics, to set a specific mood for worship, or for graphics to reinforce a story or theme, but few men (or women or teenagers for that matter) sit in worship, pencil in hand, ready to take notes off a PowerPoint® presentation.

- **The staff assumed that having the pastor encouraging the men to come to the event meant something to the men, and would make them want to come.** It usually doesn't. Pastoral leadership doesn't have the influence it once did. We live in an irreverent age, an age that doesn't admire authority. A personal invitation can be powerful, but pleas from the pulpit are seldom heard, let alone acted upon.

- **The staff assumed that men would want to come to a Bible study.** Most men don't. There was nothing in any of the advertising that told potential attendees what they would study, what it would do for them, or if it would change their lives or benefit them in any way.

- **The staff just assumed that a Bible study meant as much to the new Christians and unbelievers who attended the church as it did to the church staff.** It doesn't. Remember: The number one question people ask when they get an advertisement for anything from the church or elsewhere is, "What's in it for me?" If that question isn't answered quickly, clearly, and in a way that meets a need, people don't show up.

Some of the previous comments might seem rather unkind and somewhat brutal, or cynical. You may be thinking, "You shouldn't talk about church Bible studies that way! People do what our pastor says! I just know people are impressed with the PowerPoint® slides we make before the service starts."

I'm certain my observations aren't true in every instance. Please know that I'm not sharing these observations from a cynical heart, but from a heart that cares passionately about the church of Jesus Christ. We have to start being honest in the church about what works and about what doesn't work if we are going to market our message effectively. We are losing the hearts and souls of people to every imaginable philosophy and religion, other than a saving trust in Jesus. If some people make a decision for Christ, so often they remain baby Christians all their lives because the church doesn't seem to offer them anything more interesting than what is on TV. This has to change for the church to become the powerful, life-changing force it could be. Attempts to get people to church and involve them in activities of the church are not working very well in most cases and people must become involved in more than Sunday morning if they are to grow up in the Christian faith.

What the men's ministry planners should have done

In the example above, the church leaders needed to pray, but they also needed some marketing savvy and some common sense. They should have:

1. **Given complete information each time the event was mentioned in writing.** Remember, "the message is the message." It doesn't matter if you spend a pile of money for four-color printing if you don't give the time something starts or the location for the event.

2. **Sent out a series of postcards to the men of the church, in addition to providing the newsletter and bulletin announcements.** Postcards, if done correctly, tend to get carried directly from the mailbox to the refrigerator. Once posted, an announcement on the refrigerator is far more likely to illicit a response than an announcement in a discarded church bulletin. (Later in the book, you'll receive extensive instruction on how to make postcards effective.)

3. **Provided food.** A good, hearty, regional favorite dinner (and lots of it) at the kickoff event is an example of being market savvy.

4. **Made it an event that would appeal to unchurched men.** Starting the Bible study series with a locally popular speaker (a sports figure, perhaps) that the men would want

to come and hear would have also been a good idea. The advertising should have prominently featured the food, the speaker, and the benefits that the men would experience from the event.

These changes would have provided the Joshua contribution. The church staff still needs to pray and plan just as intensely, but the additional work of sending out some postcards and the promise of great barbecue along with the prayer makes for a Ministry Marketing victory.

Marketing misconception #3: Marketing only involves the communications created on paper or for the web

If only it were that easy, I could share with you pointers on how to create your print and web media and we'd be done with it. Even though I have lots of great ideas in those areas and thousands of wonderful examples, great-looking examples aren't the end of the story.

> *Ministry Marketing doesn't stop with our printed or web-based communications. It's part of everything we do.*

In Acts 1:8 Jesus said, "You will be my witness." Sometimes we interpret that verse as if being a witness were an option. It isn't. Individuals may be good witnesses or bad witnesses, but once a person becomes a Christian, people know. Christian behavior is judged. It's amazing how people who are not Christians have some pretty firm ideas on how Christians are supposed to act. Nobody ever says, "Oh, isn't it horrible that rock star is acting that way!" Expectations for rock stars are pretty lax. But if a Christian makes the slightest misstep, the charge of hypocrite is loudly invoked. Once someone becomes a follower of Jesus, he or she becomes a walking advertisement for the faith. For good or ill, a person's faith is judged by his or her actions.

In the same way, people have certain expectations about churches. People come to church hoping for healing and acceptance. If they meet grumpy people and messy bathrooms, they are likely to assume the Christian faith is grumpy and messy. While this may be an unfair expectation and judgment, it is reality.

Remember: Ministry Marketing consists of a "total of activities." Effective marketing is made up of many things, from signage to web sites, from postcards to e-mail, from bulletins to training programs— every imaginable communication format. Ministry Marketing spills over from the web and the printed page and into more permanent aspects of church life, including the condition of the parking lot and the availability of handicapped parking.

There will be more on this topic in the chapter *Ministry Marketing Is Pervasive*, but keep it in mind no recommendation in this book stands alone; it all goes together and it flows from who you are.

Marketing misconception #4: Marketing is costly, difficult, and for professionals who have the right equipment

In truth, effective Ministry Marketing is possible for every church, and can be done in cost-effective, relatively easy ways. Great marketing can take place in tiny churches, mega-churches, and everything in-between. It can be accomplished with pennies or thousands of dollars. The things that make it work or not (and remember, marketing that works results in changed lives) are what this book is all about.

One more part of this misconception is the belief that Ministry Marketing is successful only if marketing professionals do it. Marketing professionals can and do provide great advice and ideas, but they aren't the only source of marketing success. The difference between these two approaches is a bit like the difference between a meal cooked by a great, trained chef and one cooked by your grandmother. Professional marketing advice is like the meal produced by the trained chef. It can look picture perfect, satisfy your hunger for the exotic, and be exactly what you want. My grandmother's approach to cooking was different. She was raised on a farm and she never had a cooking class in her life. A little of this and that, hours in the kitchen, and a lot of hard work produced a Sunday dinner of Mennonite brown beef and gravy over fried potatoes, garden raised cabbage cole slaw with sweet cream dressing, homemade rolls with strawberry jam, corn and beans, bread and butter, and watermelon pickles. Strawberry and rhubarb pie topped with sugar and cream and dark, strong coffee finished the meal.

There's more than one way to fill a tummy, and more than one way to approach successful Ministry Marketing.

Your Ministry Marketing may take the professional chef's approach, with slick, glossy publications and a big marketing budget. Or you may go the grandma path—a little of this and that, hours on the computer, and a lot of hard work that produces your own materials. Either way can work.

CHAPTER 3:

Unworthy and Worthy Marketing Purposes

You have a motivation, a purpose, for all of the marketing you do in your church. You may never have taken the time to define it or you may not even be aware of it, but your purpose in publications and marketing, what motivates you, is the unspoken guide for all you do.

To be successful in Ministry Marketing, please take time to define and understand your purposes and commit to worthy ones. Following is an example of what can happen if you don't take time to define the purpose and motivation behind the marketing activities in your ministry.

Ministry Marketing sabotaged by an unspoken purpose

Hilltop Church really wanted to improve its Ministry Marketing, but even after seminar trainings, reading books, and some time spent in one-on-one consulting, few changes were taking place. Its communication pieces were boring and bland. In spite of repeated examples, ideas, and suggestions for improvement, nothing changed. The church had a new pastor and the leadership talked loudly about wanting to reach

I want you to think about what marketing isn't . . . At best, marketing can convince people of an obvious truth. At worst, it often fails to even accomplish this feat. Marketing certainly does not have the power to make lies come true.[9]

Marketing is the most important thing you do in business today . . . This is true because marketing, in all its varied forms, is concerned with attracting customers, getting them to buy, and making sure they are happy enough with their purchase that they come back for more. What could be more important? Ever try to run a business without customers?[10]
    —Alexander Hiam,
      Marketing for Dummies

unchurched people, but the church's publications were seriously out of touch with what could work for its intended audience.

In an effort to discover the source of the problem, I had lunch with the office manager. I knew that what ends up in the publications that reach people in the pews is not so much what the church leadership decides they want, but what the support staff believes it should do. I decided to meet with the church office manager, Jean, to discover the belief system at work in the hearts of the publication team.

Between bites of salad, I asked, "If you had to define the driving purpose, the motivating force behind all the communications you put out in the church, what would it be?"

She thought before answering and then said, "Well, I think if I had to pick the most important motivation or driving force behind all our communications, as far as the church staff is concerned, it would be, 'Don't ever put anything out with a typo in it.'"

"Oh my," I said. I wasn't sure how to respond.

Producing materials free of typographical errors is a worthy goal, but it is not a tremendously motivating goal. Negative standards (don't do this or that) will never inspire much creativity or passion. I now understood at least part of the reason why the church's promotional materials hadn't changed in over ten years. They were typo-free, certainly, but also boring, full of insider jargon, and largely ineffective.

What is the purpose that motivates the publications ministry of your church?

Take time to figure it out. Creating successful Ministry Marketing and publications is difficult, demanding, and time-consuming work. You don't want unspoken purposes to keep you from being less successful than you can be. Before I give you what I call the *Three Worthy Purposes for Ministry Marketing*, I'd like to share some of the *Unworthy Motivating Purposes* I have observed.

Unworthy Purpose #1: Keep the sanctuary tidy

It's amazing how many church communication and marketing programs are governed by neatness—not neatness in the publications, but neatness in the church building. Neatness here means that the goal for Sunday morning communication has nothing to do with what is actually printed or handed out. The primary goal is that no stray papers are ever to be left on the floor after the Sunday morning service. To make certain this does not happen, no bulletin inserts are allowed. That means no reminders to people of events, no sermon notes, no registration or prayer cards, no children's bulletins, youth news, or national church updates are allowed.

Not including these pieces of essential information is a huge marketing mistake. Bulletin inserts, designed like mini-billboards to advertise upcoming events, get posted on the refrigerator, and people attend the events. Separate sermon notes greatly increase the potential retention of the pastor's message. Children's bulletins can make the difference between a church service being fun or being a trial for a child.

Allowing the communications ministry of the church to be governed by unrealistic standards of church tidiness is shortsighted. Churches that do this forget that "sheep" are messy.

> *Good pastors realize that if they want to meet the needs of the sheep (their congregation) it won't always be the tidiest process, and that may mean some stray pieces of paper on the floor.*

Unworthy Purpose #2:
Marketing needs to look like the publications produced by our hero church

This usually becomes the guiding purpose for people who work in church publications and marketing after the senior pastor or other members of the leadership team attend a national church growth conference. They return, clutching samples of the big church's publications, and plop them on the desk of the church secretary. "Have these made for us by Sunday," they command. The unspoken assumption is that if we create marketing and publications like the big church does, then we will be a big church, too. It doesn't work that way.

First of all, smaller churches usually don't have the software, hardware, training, or budget to reproduce what mega-churches produce. To ask church staff to create similar publications without adequate resources is an exercise in frustration.

Secondly, even if the mega-church publications could be replicated, a church of 100 that sends out a piece that looks like it comes from a big, high-budget ministry is literally practicing false advertising.

I observed one sad example of this involving a small, start-up church. The church of about fifty people met in a community center. The church that sponsored this new church convinced them they needed to send out full-color, slick, printed flyers created by a professional advertising agency to bring newcomers into the church. The publication cost so much the church couldn't pay the pastor, but they felt this was what they needed to do to attract visitors. When people did show up for worship based on the mailer (and there weren't many who responded), most visitors were surprised that a group that looked so professional on paper was so small in person. Most of the visitors didn't return.

The word "small" is not a bad word when used to describe either your church or your church's publications. Many people don't want to go to a big church. Most people don't expect a small or start-up church to create fancy publications. If the publications are too fancy, visitors will probably think the church is spending too much money on them—and the church probably is.

Be sure your publications honestly reflect who you are. They should look like they come from your church, not the church that sponsored the latest seminar.

Unworthy purpose #3:
We've always done it that way

Often cited as the battle cry of a dying church, this statement has a huge effect on the success or failure of communications and marketing.

The church bulletin is the Ministry Marketing publication that most often falls victim to this maxim. You may never have thought of your church bulletin as a marketing publication before, but it is one of the most important marketing pieces produced by the church. For people in today's post-Christian world, church bulletins are often the first piece of Christian literature they ever see. Certainly, it is their first introduction to your church. What does it say to them?

Many church bulletins start out with a picture of the church on the cover. This has always struck me as odd, because we know what the church looks like—we are sitting in it. Open the bulletin and newcomers find words like *Introit, Invocation, Offertory, Prelude, Postlude,* and various other church terms and events. Few if any of these words are explained. The bulletin is filled with announcements about AWANAs, the Going Concern, the Growing Edge, the Becomers, and the Mariners. A visitor can't begin to guess what these names describe. The budget is often included and a plea for increased giving can be found. None of this content speaks to searching souls. The main message of the bulletin to an unchurched seeker is, "This is an insider club and you don't belong."

Numerous statistical studies show that approximately seventy percent of people who visit churches do not come back a second time.

Churches don't mean to turn people away with publications, but "if we've always done it that way" is expressed as a reason behind how the bulletin and other publications are created, there is a good chance that this in some way contributes to the return of visitors.

I think this is one of the saddest statistics in the church today, but if we want to change it, we have to look at the part our publications play in turning away people who are coming to church for answers. This book will inspire you to reverse that situation.

Unworthy purpose #4: We must do it with excellence, or we won't do it at all

Excellence in this case is a variation on the no-typo goal talked about above, but the issue goes deeper than typos and gets into matters of design, layout, and typefaces. The belief that churches should only produce works of excellence is often held by someone who attended a design conference or by a church volunteer who is a also a professional designer.

Once again, I have nothing against good design. I love clean, clear, quality design. I can discuss for hours the joys of white space and the beauty of serifs on well-cut typefaces. But what does that have to do with ninety percent of the publications produced by the church office? If a program like MS Publisher® is used, and the office worker makes good use of the templates, then acceptable design is guaranteed.

For Ministry Marketing publications, great design is the icing on the cake, not the deciding factor that determines whether or not the cake should be made.

I have never heard a person being baptized testify, "You know, it was the typeface that drew me to Jesus." I've never heard anyone say, "The lack of white space on the invitation hardened my heart so I didn't go to the church picnic."

If you are a newly single mom, you probably don't care what the church publication looks like that advertises an event for singles and their kids. All that matters is that you get a postcard that tells you what time the event starts, what it costs (hopefully free) and if child-care is provided (hopefully free also).

Many of the Ministry Marketing pieces that will have the greatest impact on the lives of people are the ones that don't worry about excellence, but are instead, good enough.

Good enough means:

- Good enough gets the postcards out in time, realizing that the basic facts of time, location, directions, and contact phone number are more important than expensive printing.

- Good enough realizes that a simple flyer for the refrigerator every week as a reminder of youth activities might work better than the professionally printed piece that is put out every quarter.

- Good enough realizes that adding a couple of extra pages to the newsletter in order to include details for people unfamiliar with the church is more important than using a more expensive paper.

- Good enough means missing a typo is acceptable so the church office worker can go home at a decent hour and spend some time with his or her family, instead of proofing the brochure one more time.

Unworthy also means unsatisfying

In addition to being unworthy from a ministry viewpoint, the purposes above are usually unsatisfying in terms of ministry results. People aren't dumb. They can tell if a church cares more about how a publication looks than the completeness of the information it contains. People can tell if a church cares more about maintaining traditions than making certain visitors are comfortable with the worship service.

Worthy Purposes

There is nothing original about the worthy Ministry Marketing purposes that follow. Each of them is based on the Bible and each is used in a variety of successful church growth programs today. Ginghamsburg United Methodist Church, Saddleback, Willow Creek, and many others have their own ways of restating these purposes. Since I've been to many of these churches' workshops and read their books, my mind mixes together quite a bit of what they've said. Without trying to sort out what came from whom and what I came up with on my own, I want to acknowledge them as the source of much inspiration for the following worthy purposes.[11]

> Then Jesus came to them and said, "All authority in heaven and on earth has been given to me. Therefore go and make disciples of all nations, baptizing them in the name of the Father and of the Son and of the Holy Spirit, and teaching them to obey everything I have commanded you. And surely I am with you always, to the very end of the age."
> —Matthew 28:18-20, NIV

The three worthy purposes that should guide Ministry Marketing are:

The Great Commission

The Great Commandment

The Great Goal

Though these driving purposes are not the only worthy purposes you can have in Ministry Marketing, they are important to keep in mind because they are the essential basics needed to accomplish the spiritual goals of your church.

Worthy Purpose #1: The Great Commission

The Great Commission should be the foundational motivation for everything we do in Ministry Marketing. It is not the great suggestion. It is the true north by which we steer our life. It is the canon by which we measure everything we do, including all our Ministry Marketing.

Easy to affirm; difficult to implement

Most people would agree that the Great Commission should be the basis for all we do as a church, including church marketing and publications. But sometimes reality is not that simple. In one of my seminars, an honest pastor raised his hand and asked, "But what if my church really doesn't care? What if they aren't concerned about the Great Commission and feel that the church exists primarily to serve the people already there?"

That was a great question and one you must answer before you start any Ministry Marketing program.

If your church isn't where you want it to be in relation to the Great Commission, you may want to do some preliminary teaching on the subject before you introduce it as a foundational purpose for Ministry Marketing. However, as important as a commitment to the Great Commission is, don't wait until everyone is convinced before allowing it to motivate you.

> *When the members of your church see changed lives, it's amazing how motivating that can be.*

As an example of this dynamic, in one of my current favorite books, *Blue Like Jazz*, the author shares this story:

> After I got Laura's e-mail in which she told me she had become a Christian I just about lost it with excitement. I felt like a South African the day they let Mandela out of prison. I called her . . . She said we had much to talk about, very much to talk about . . . even though Laura had been my close friend, I felt like I had never met this woman. She squirmed in her seat as she talked with confidence about her love for Jesus. I sat there amazed because it is true. People do come to know Jesus. This crazy thing really happens.[12]

I get excited every time I read that passage. Sometimes people have to see the Great Commission in action before they decide to become involved. Form a team and get started. When your church sees people coming to know Jesus, the excitement will be contagious and your church will grow.

Worthy Purpose #2: The Great Commandment

1 Corinthians 13 says that if we communicate in the most expensive and elaborate way possible ("with the tongues of men and angels"), if we don't com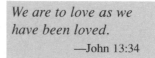municate with love, we're just making noise. In contrast, it has been my experience that people doing communications work in the church often do a great job of communicating with love, even though their marketing publications may not meet some secular marketing standards.

We are to love as we have been loved.
—John 13:34

I saw a great example of this when, at one of my seminars, a Methodist preacher came up to me at the break and showed me her church bulletin. She had gone into the ministry as a second career and was pastoring in her first church, a small church in the country. From a "design" viewpoint her bulletin would not have won any awards. But you could see that she loved her people.

The bulletin outlined a traditional Methodist service, with the prelude and other "church" words listed, but below each one the pastor explained what it meant. For example, under *Prelude* she wrote, "As you come in we play some quiet music. Just sit down and let your heart relax before we start the service." Under *Invocation* she said, "Here, we'll talk to God. I'll lead, but He is your Father too, so talk to Him about whatever you want." And it went on like that throughout the whole bulletin. It was wonderful.

"Did you put these in here?" I asked. "Yeah," she replied. "You know I got to thinking—none of my folks know what those big words mean."

"Is your little church growing?" I asked.

She smiled, "It is."

Her love for her people made her a good communicator. She got to know them and learned about their lives. She didn't take a seminar on "Contextualizing the Liturgical Message for the Rural Congregation." She just loved her folks and talked to them in a language she knew they would understand.

Loving your people is one of the best forms of marketing research you can do.

Put pictures of people from your congregation by your computer as you work—talk directly to them as you create your communication pieces. Walk the neighborhood you want to reach and pray for insight on how to reach the people who live there. Look at the local publications, magazines, and newspapers your target audience reads. Create materials for *your* people—you know them best.

Worthy Purpose #3: The Great Goal

Present every believer mature [perfect, complete] in Christ.
—Colossians 1:28

Most churches give up on Ministry Marketing and communication too soon. Churches give up too soon in how much marketing needs to be done and how many pieces and repetitions it takes in today's media-saturated world to make an impact. It takes a huge amount of work to promote specific events. But even more important, most Ministry Marketing stops short in its expectation for results that should be reflected in people's lives.

People need to learn the entire story of the gospel message. They need to be equipped when challenges and troubles come. They need to know the end of the story so they aren't discouraged in difficult times. Many people become disillusioned with the Christian faith because they confuse the gospel story with the story of how to get rich quick in America, or the story of how power and fame assure a happy ending.

In order for people to mature in their faith, they need to be involved in activities in your church that facilitate Christian maturity.

Your goal is not only to share the gospel story with people, but also to help them learn the story well enough to become storytellers themselves.

That takes time and involvement with your church—involvement that goes beyond Sunday morning.

Marketing should be about more than Sunday morning

The focus of much of Christian marketing today is on getting people to the Sunday morning service. That's an important focus, but it is only the first step on the road to Christian maturity. There is much more that needs to happen for people to become, as Willow Creek Church says, "fully devoted followers of Christ."

To do that, your Ministry Marketing needs to shift from external marketing to internal marketing. You need to work just as hard to get people to the small groups, Christian growth seminars, recovery classes, and adult training as you do to get them involved in the Sunday morning service.

We'll expand on the idea of doing more than marketing Sunday morning in the next section.

CHAPTER 4:

The Three Ministry Marketing Killer Assumptions

Even though your church may have worthy marketing purposes in place, you may still need to rid yourself of three key Ministry Marketing killers. Many churches practice these killers unconsciously and in doing so sabotage much marketing work and waste a lot of money.

Ministry Marketing Killer Assumption #1:
The Sunday service is the only church event we need to advertise

Put yourself in the place of the average American person who is interested in finding out something about God. Just by virtue of growing up in our society, where would you go? What day and what time would you go?

Some objections to "marketing ministry" seem to be based on the misconception that to do strategic planning and purposeful marketing is to take matters out of God's hands and place them in our own . . . to rely on human wisdom instead of God's. Nothing could be further from the truth. Marketing strategy in ministry seeks God's strategy.[13]
—George Barna,
Church Marketing:
Breaking the Ground for
Ministry

The most obvious answer, of course, is to a church. Though the time may vary somewhat, you'll probably be ninety-nine percent accurate if you show up at any church, any Sunday, between 9:00 a.m. and noon. If you visit a church then, you'll find something about God happening.

However, what if you're looking for other activities? When do children or teenage groups meet? Where does the single's group meet? What about small group Bible studies? What about recovery groups? If you want to meet other men who want to live and work with integrity, if you want to grow in your faith, when and where do these events take place?

The when and where answers for these events are not obvious. Specific age, gender, and topical events take place at a variety of times and in a variety of places in the life of the church. They are different for every church and sometimes change from month to month, and even week to week.

> *Every activity in the church, with the possible exception of the Sunday morning worship service, requires intentional, repeated, and consistent marketing to your intended audience and congregation.*

The reason many churches have large turnouts for Sunday and small turnouts for other activities is that churches spend the majority of time, effort, and money on the one event that needs the least advertising. Churches spend almost no time, effort, or money on the events that need advertising the most.

Ministry Marketing Killer Assumption #2: Everybody knows what's going on

Church communicators often say, "Oh, everybody knows about . . ." the kids' club, Mom's morning out, the women's group, or whatever other ministry of the local church. The assumption that everybody already knows all the details of all the events in the church is the reason given for not getting out more information about events outside of Sunday morning worship. However, the reality is that everybody doesn't know.

One of the occupational hazards of vocational ministry is that those of us who work in the church office or on the staff assume that the activities and ministries of our church are as important to church members as they are to us. People are not as focused on them as we are. We assume that people know all the ministry times, locations, and contact phone numbers as well as we do, but they don't.

If you question the truth of this statement, try the following exercise some Sunday morning. Have a blank sheet of paper in the bulletin. Tell people that the church will provide brunch at the nicest restaurant in town for the entire family, (don't worry, you won't have to actually do it) if anyone can list all of the activities going on at the church during the upcoming week. Ask them to write down where the groups meet, what time they start and end, and the name, contact phone number, and e-mail of the person in charge of each event.

At the end of this exercise you will receive a lot of totally blank pieces of paper. People do not know what's going on in their church. Even if they have a vague idea that the church does some sort of small group thing, for example, often they don't know the details that are important for their own involvement.

> *You've got to provide detailed information and repeat it frequently or people won't show up.*

If people don't show up, they won't grow in the faith.

Ministry Marketing Killer Assumption #3: Everybody hears our message as often as we share it

Church workers plan events or educational experience for the people of the church for months, but often they wait until the last minute before they think about letting the congregation in on what is happening. Do not wait until the last minute to include the congregation. So much work goes into preparation and planning that by the time the church staff finally works out all of the details and it is time to advertise the event, the staff is sick to death of even thinking about it. For the church staff, this is the time when advertising work needs to be done intentionally and repeatedly.

The secret to Ministry Marketing

Remember: sharing the gospel, loving people, and helping them grow in the faith are the worthy purposes for Ministry Marketing. Finding ways to live out these purposes is what the rest of the book is about.

Before I get into the specifics, I'd like to share an important little secret I have learned from interacting with thousands of folks who do marketing and communications in the church. If you choose the three purposes mentioned above, overcome the three killer assumptions, and if, out of love for your people, you really want to do marketing for the glory of God, *you cannot fail.*

It doesn't matter how good you are with a computer. It doesn't matter if you don't know a display typeface from a readable text font. It doesn't matter how old your equipment is or what software you have. It doesn't matter if you are young or mature, if you've worked at the church for forty years, or you are just getting started. If you care enough to do your best with whatever tools you've been given, wherever you are and whoever you are, if you give it to Jesus—you will be successful.

It's kind of like the little boy with the five fish and a bit of bread. It wasn't much in his hands, but when he put his lunch into the big hands of the Carpenter, great things happened.

The hands of the Carpenter are now nail-scarred, but if you place your Ministry Marketing projects into them, he will take them and multiply their effect beyond your wildest dreams. Ministry Marketing really is easy with Jesus working beside you and through you.

CHAPTER 5:

Characteristics of Ministry Marketing Audiences

It's much easier to get your message across if you know to whom you are talking. We structure messages differently to third-grade audiences as opposed to senior citizens. Every successful marketing program is an expansion of this idea. Good Ministry Marketing begins by doing all you can to understand your target audience.

When he saw the crowds, he had compassion on them, because they were harassed and helpless, like sheep without a shepherd.
—Matthew 9:36, NIV

While many characteristics describe the church's ministry audience, we will limit our discussion to seven key characteristics. These characteristics define the lives of people both inside and outside the church. It's important to identify and understand these characteristics because most of them did not characterize the church's ministry audiences a few years ago. If you are communicating with an outdated vision of your ministry audience, your Ministry Marketing will be a constant exercise in frustration.

Not long ago people were less busy, respected authority, knew when a reference was made to something out of the Bible, believed science held the answers to the wrongs of the world, and held to standards of right and wrong. You can't count on any of these beliefs being present in the church's audience today.

These Seven Key Characteristics of Ministry Marketing Audiences will show that church audiences generally are:

- authority-indifferent
- time-starved
- live in a post-Christian world

- without a collective church consciousness

- spiritually searching

- postmodern, at least in part

- diverse.

Your Audience Is Authority-Indifferent

"As America has been rocked by financial and sexual scandals in the past several months, resulting in a collapse of public confidence in leaders and a serious financial collapse on Wall Street, the public is triangulated in its response to recent shenanigans: some are ambivalent, many are angry, and millions are interested in back-to-the-basics reforms . . . people's reactions run the gamut from hostility to indifference—but that few Americans retain a high level of trust in the leading cultural influencers."[14]
—Barna Research Online

In the past, if an announcement or a letter came to the house from the church, it was opened and read with respect, especially if it was from the pastor. You can't count on that response today, and it isn't the pastor's fault. It's due to a general leveling down of respect for authority throughout our society. Through the media we have seen images of corrupt cops, immoral clergy, cheating business leaders, and temper-tantrum-throwing politicians.

The Internet has made anyone with a bad attitude an instant authority. There is a commentator on every cable and network channel who, speaking with authority one week, is the subject of a scandalous expose the next week. When anyone can be an authority and little of that authority is respected, it affects the way Ministry Marketing publications are received and should affect how they are created.

Practical tips for relating to authority-indifferent audiences

- Don't assume anything you create will be read just because it's coming from your church and your position of authority.

- Instead of authority as a basis for assuring people will read your message, base communication on the building of relationships. The statement, "People don't care how much you know until they know how much you care" is the formula for successful communication today. If people don't like you, they won't pay attention to any communication from you.

- Think in terms of "we are offering this to you because we care" not "you'd better do this because I say you have to."

Your Audience Is Time-Starved

Based on the quote from *The Wall Street Journal*, Dale McFeatters notes that, on average, Americans spend fifty-three hours a week working. He then factors in the statistics for the various other activities of life. Worship was included as part of the 46.9-hour block that also included "exercise and sports, in transit and caring for children and pets."[16] Activities such as sleeping, eating, and time spent watching television were in another category. After adding together the totals for each category, McFeatters concludes that we need a week of 196.5 hours (a seven-day week has only 168 hours) to get done all

The battle for Americans' disposable time—among a vast proliferation of entertainment products and media channels—is becoming even more pitched than the battle for their disposable income. Indeed in many key demographic groups, time is scarcer than money.[15]

—The Wall Street Journal

the things we say we do each week. "We now have a 28.5-hour time deficit," said McFeatters. "In other words, at the end of the weekend, you are more than a full day behind in your activities. Even if we went to an eight-day week you still would be 4.5 hours behind."

This may sound humorous, but it really isn't. Life is overly full and highly stressful today for everyone. If people are not reading and responding to what you try to communicate from your church or ministry, it isn't because they have lost interest in church or hate God and have abandoned their faith. Most often it is because people are simply too busy.

Practical tips for communicating to time-starved people

- Just because what you have to say is important, you do not need to use multiple pages to say it. Keep your marketing communications short and to the point. John 3:16 is only twenty-five words long.

- Let CNN's Headline News slogan inspire you: "Real News, Real Fast." Give your people significant information and give it to them in a format that can be quickly read and understood immediately.

- Use postcards. I'm a huge advocate of postcards, and for good reason. Postcards are one of the best ways to communicate almost every Ministry Marketing message. They are a great way to communicate to busy people who won't take the time to open an envelope and read a lengthy publication. Postcards should be used for short notices, reminders, and anything that can potentially be posted on the refrigerator. Postcards on refrigerators enable busy people respond because all the action information is right there.

- The Direct Mail Marketing Association reports that forty-four percent of bulk mail is never opened. Communicate in ways that don't require opening an envelope, including the use of e-mail, door-hangers, and postcards.

- Make the most of e-mail messages. Always put a summary of your message in the subject line for people who only skim the subjects in their inbox. For example, instead of writing "Important Event at Church Tonight," summarize the exact details. For example, say, "Men's BBQ and Coach Bradley to Speak at 6" or "Bring Munchies, a friend, five bucks to Youth Lock-in Friday."

Your Audience Lives in a Post-Christian Culture

Many of us no longer live in a Christian nation—that's the world we all live in no matter what our belief system may be. There are two key results that affect you as a Ministry Marketer because of this.

- Sunday is no longer a sacred day.

- Society no longer has a collective church consciousness.

> *Theology does not occur within a vacuum—the changing times Bob Dylan sang about have swept through theology as well, breaking down the traditional lines and categories changing the way theology is done . . . The great theological task today is to rethink the "message"—to contextualize the gospel for the postmodern world.*[17]
>
> —Craig Detweiler and Barry Taylor

Implications of Sunday no longer being a sacred day

The fact that Sunday is no longer sacred affects both the people you are trying to reach outside your church and the people in your church. People from both groups often have to work on Sunday. In addition, many schools hold athletic and other events on Sunday. Not everyone you want to reach can come to church on Sunday, even if they want to. Not everyone who is a member of your church can attend every Sunday.

Lyle Schaller tells us that only twenty percent of church members attend worship every Sunday of any given month. Thirty percent are there two to three Sundays out of the month, while twenty percent are there one Sunday a month. A full thirty percent of church members cannot be there on Sunday.[18]

Yet, despite these facts, most churches conduct their communications efforts as if everyone who is interested in what they offer, or might at any time be interested, attends church every Sunday. Attendance assumptions do not reflect current reality, and many messages are printed and delivered so infrequently that much of the intended audience never sees them.

Practical application to communicating to church members

- If the primary way you communicate to church members is through the Sunday morning bulletin, thirty to eighty percent of your church members never find out what is going on. Many of those folks may be interested in coming to something at the church during the week, if only they are made aware of what is happening.

- Institute ways to communicate with people outside of the Sunday morning bulletin. Reach them with information about events, even if you may consider it boring, "everybody knows" news items. This will help keep people who cannot attend on Sunday morning informed. Consider a postcard or e-mail update with a summary of event information for the week sent out to every member. Track the results and if you see a greater turnout at events, it might be a good practice to continue.

- The automatic solution is not to put the bulletin on the Internet every week and expect people to take the initiative to check it out. That might be part of the solution, but it isn't the total answer. Not every church has the ability to post communications on the web, and not every church member has online access.

- Consider doing a congregational survey to determine the best way to inform your people. In addition to trying some of the above suggestions, ask people how they want to receive information and let them choose between e-mail, printed newsletter, postcard, or a combination of them all. Ask them to suggest alternatives. Try various methods, record your results, and continue the practices that consistently bring in the most people.

Your Audience Has No Collective Church Consciousness[19]

Realizing that today's audience has no collective church consciousness means that when we use church language, people often don't know what we're talking about. They did not grow up in school reading the Bible and they don't hear about it from secular media. Because the church doesn't speak the same language as the rest of the world, you may need to modify some of your outreach language.

You may be thinking, "I know that. I know better than to use terms like sanctification and justification in my outreach brochure. I'm even careful about how I use the term saved." While that may be true, I find that most church communicators are shocked at just how deep this lack of a collective church consciousness runs when they take time to find out what it really implies.

> *Secular men and women . . . don't generally come to Christ in one fell swoop. They don't hear one good sermon, read one solid Christian book, have one strategic spiritual conversation, or go to one knockout seeker event, and then decide on the spot to repent of their sins and turn their lives to God.*[20]
> —Mark Mittelberg,
>   Building a Contagious Church

George Barna has some interesting statistics. He tells us that seven out of ten adults have no idea what John 3:16 means.[21] From my own personal experience, I've learned that not only does that mean that people can't quote the verse (which some have called the most loved verse in the Bible), they don't even know it *is* a Bible verse.

I remember seeing this illustrated a number of years ago during the Super Bowl. John Elway was the quarterback. At one point during the game, a young man rolled out a big banner as the television camera panned his way. The banner read, "John 3:16." The sportscaster covering the Super Bowl saw the banner and made a comment something like this, "John 3, 16. Now that's a statistic of Elway's I'm not familiar with." He was not being a smart aleck. He didn't know John 3:16 was a verse from the Bible and neither do seventy percent of the people you want to reach with the gospel message.

The American public in general does not know what the names, words, and code numbers that comprise verse references mean. It is a mistake for churches to put them in marketing publications.

Another statistic important to remember in Ministry Marketing is this: when non-Christians where asked why Christians celebrate Easter, forty-six percent could not give an accurate answer.[22] Most people who did not grow up in the church associate Easter with chocolate bunnies and Cadbury eggs.

Practical tips for communicating to people who do not have a collective church consciousness

- It is important to write out Bible verses if you are using them in any sort of seeker-friendly church service or outreach. To simply list Bible verse references and expect unchurched people to look them up later, or even know what you are talking about, is not realistic. Obviously you'll want to use a more contemporary Bible translation. Check out www.biblegateway.com for an easy way to find verses in all the contemporary translations and cut and paste them into your outreach publications.

- Even more than at Christmas, we need to remind people "Jesus is the Reason for the Season" at Easter. Most people still know that Christmas has something to do with Jesus' birth, even if they do not accept its significance. With Easter, many people honestly don't know anything about its religious significance. Remember that before you take out a big ad inviting people to your Easter cantata. "What's the big deal?" might be the response of many people. Knowing this reality, many churches now call their Easter service Resurrection Sunday. That lets people know what is being celebrated.

- Be careful about using Bible analogies or allusions in any teaching, even at church, unless you have a good idea of the how familiar your audience is with the Bible. Always include explanations and appropriate background. Many seeker-friendly churches are great about not using Christian jargon in outreach, but they forget that Bible knowledge does not come automatically with conversion. Newly converted people may have no idea what you are talking about when you mention loaves and fish, manna and quail, or cherubim and seraphim.

Your Audience Is Very Spiritual

Sarah Pike's comments concerning New-Age spirituality deal with just one segment of the abundance of spiritual options available in the world today. We live in a very spiritual world, full of belief in gods and goddesses, growing participation in traditional world religions such as Islam, and a proliferation of current cults. Spirituality is everywhere, but be careful how you apply this observation in your Ministry Marketing.

Just because people are spiritual does not mean they are interested in Christianity. Just because someone prays, or says that he or she believes in God, do not immediately assume he or she uses these terms in the same way you do. At the same time, it is exciting to see that many people today are more open to exploring spiritual matters than they were a few years ago when a more rational, scientific, fact-oriented mindset was dominate.

> *From Shirley MacLaine's motion picture spiritual biography* Out on a Limb *to the teenage witches in the film,* The Craft, *New Age and Neopagan beliefs have made sensationalistic headlines . . . Self-help books by New Age channelers and psychics are a large and growing market; annual spending on channeling, self-help businesses, and alternative health care is at $10 to $14 billion; an estimated 12 million Americans are involved with New Age activities; and American Neopagans are estimated at around 80,000-100,000.*[23]
> —Sarah Pike

Because people are interested in spirituality, but not necessarily Christian spirituality, many Christians have no idea where to start a conversation, let alone how to begin Ministry Marketing to this audience. The following are some suggestions for how to address this problem.

Old marketing suggestions for the new situation

As the Bible says, " . . . there is nothing new under the sun" (Eccles. 9:1) and in this instance, I think of two people who can help guide our dialogue and marketing approaches with spiritual, but not yet Christian, people today. The first guide is the Apostle Paul and the second guide is C. S. Lewis. Both these men valued a heart searching for spiritual meaning. They did not choose to destroy an opposing spirituality; they used the spirituality of their audience as a bridge to share the full story of the gospel message.

In Acts 17, when Paul went around Athens looking at the pagan idols, reading Athenian inscriptions, and memorizing their poetry, he did not shout: "Abomination, abomination!" Instead, he took time to understand their spirituality and then used their interest in idols as a bridge to sharing the gospel message.

C.S. Lewis does similar things in many of his writings. Since childhood, he loved mythology and went on to become a professor of Classics. When he became a Christian later in life, he did not discard the spiritual, mythological interests of his youth. He valued them for the truths he saw inside every myth, truths that hint at the true story. As he puts it:

> . . . myth is the isthmus which connects the peninsular world of thought with that vast continent we really belong to. It is not, like truth, abstract: nor is it, like direct experience, bound to the particular . . . The heart of Christianity is a myth which is also a fact. The old myth of the Dying God, without ceasing to be myth, comes down from the heaven of legend and imagination to the earth of history. It happens—at a particular date, in a particular place, followed by definable historical consequences. We pass from a Balder or an Osiris, dying nobody knows when or where, to a historical Person crucified (it is all in order) under Pontius Pilate. By becoming fact it does not cease to be myth: that is the miracle.[24]

If we approach the world today in the manner of St. Paul and C. S. Lewis, Ministry Marketing can take on a creative and exciting approach. People from every walk of life are screaming out interest in God. While they don't have all of the details, they are telling the parts of the story that they do know in their media, their music, and other outlets for their spiritual expression. Many searching people know that we are created to live for a purpose greater than ourselves, that something outside ourselves guides the events of life, that souls exist beyond death, that whoever or however the Creator is defined, that entity desires goodness, kindness, and sometimes sacrifice on behalf of fellow humans.

Good Ministry Marketing applauds these beliefs as steps towards truth and creatively uses them as bridges to sharing the full story of the Christian faith.

Practical applications in Ministry Marketing to today's spirituality

- One of the most important things that persons in Ministry Marketing can do is look and listen to the world with a prayerful attitude, listening below the surface of the multitude of stories for what is in people's hearts. Ask God for respect, love, and insight for people who practice a spirituality that is not Christian.

- Ask the Lord to give you insight into the questions really being asked and how you may use these in Ministry Marketing. A good practice is to go to movies, watch popular television shows, and work to figure out the underlying spiritual beliefs and needs presented. Use these as a bridge to sharing the truth.

For example, John Edwards is a popular psychic who appears regularly on Larry King and has a television show called *Crossing Over*. While there are several verses in scripture that say mediums should be put to death, handing out a copy of the verses and inviting the unchurched of your community to a seminar called "The Devil's Deceptions in Prime Time Media" might not bring in a lot of seekers.

Instead, consider another approach. First, look at what motivates people who watch John Edwards. He is hugely popular because people want to know what happens after death. They want to be assured that their loved ones aren't blotted out of existence when their eyes close on earth. The messages John Edwards gives are vague, and even though sometimes correct details are hit upon, ultimately the message is unsatisfying and incomplete. For people who are spiritually hungry, the answers given by psychics are partial at best. People who turn to them only hear myths and lies.

The Christian gospel tells the whole story. A more positive approach to dealing with psychic deception is one taken by First Presbyterian Church in Colorado Springs. My mother attended that church. For many years, on the Sunday after Easter, senior minister John Stevens preached a glorious, hope-filled message on life after death from the Christian perspective. The church was always full and people responded.

- Sometimes you don't have time to share the whole story, but even then you have the opportunity to acknowledge the spiritual motive behind the people's questions. Look for ways to begin a conversation others might finish. In marketing terms when you do this you build product awareness.

I had a chance to "build product awareness" for Jesus on a plane trip a while ago. I happened to be reading my Bible during the flight. People often comment when they see me doing that. It's as if I have a big target on my forehead and anyone who has a grudge against God interprets it as permission to take aim. The gentleman next to me obviously had not had very happy experiences with the Christian church. However, environmentalism was important to him and he wanted to know why God allowed such awful things to be done to the earth.

I responded that God didn't intend for the destruction that was happening to take place on earth. I shared that God created the world to be perfect and good, and that God intended for humanity to take care of it, but sin entered the world and we messed it all up. I told him sin harmed all of creation, not just people. But I told him that God did something about the existence of harmful sin and that one day, not only people, but all of creation would be renewed.

He answered quietly, "I've never heard that. That's a wonderful thought." I would have liked us to have continued our conversation, but at that moment it was time to get off the plane.

- Remind yourself that you aren't the only storyteller of the gospel message.

After that plane conversation, I felt terribly guilty that I wasn't able to whip out a little gospel tract and in five minutes lead the seeking environmentalist in a prayer of repentance. But maybe, I told myself, I started a conversation and began the story that the Lord will lead another brother or sister to continue. Maybe, if others tell their parts of the story whenever they get the chance, I'll see that man again when all things are renewed.

Parts of Your Audience Are Postmodern

I intentionally emphasize the word "parts" because the audience for Ministry Marketing is diverse: some are postmodern, and some are not.

The term *postmodern* is used a lot these days in theological and outreach discussions, but many people (including many church leaders) have a hard time figuring out what it means. That's okay,

> *Moderns liked to draw up lists of principles for which they were willing to die. Postmoderns draw up lists of practices we are willing to live by.*[25]
> —Leonard Sweet, *Soul Salsa*

because you don't need to understand all that the term encompasses to be aware of its effect on Ministry Marketing. What is important to understand is that, for persons with postmodern mindsets, there are no absolutes, no ultimate truths, and no infallible authorities. If beliefs cannot be lived in reality, then they are not real and even then they are only real to the person who believes them.

Postmodern thought applied to marketing and evangelism means many seekers coming to your church don't approach truth in ways that it was approached in the past. For example, many baby boomers learned to arrive at theological conclusions by asserting scientific, logical proofs (a la Josh McDowell, and others). This generation was taught to argue its position clearly and expect people to respond rationally. A different approach is appropriate for the postmodern. Postmodern people in general cannot be argued into the kingdom.

Instead, Postmodern Ministry Marketing does these things:

- It tells the gospel story.

- It invites people to come into the gospel story, to join other people in a spiritual journey or dance, and to join in the activities of the family of faith.

- In the context of community, it lives out the gospel story. The truth is seen in action, not just in words.

- It patiently waits, it answers questions, it provides opportunities for non-threatening involvement with the Christian community.

Brian McLaren illustrates this approach when he talks about his church being a place where "people can belong before they believe."[26] He goes on to say, "*Sometimes belonging must precede believing*" (McLaren's italics). In other words, unless we let not-as-yet-Christians enter and participate in the Christian community, many of them won't become Christians. This approach reflects Jesus' own example. He was criticized for being a friend of sinners because he welcomed and accepted people who did not yet believe right, think right, speak right, or act right. But Jesus knew something we need to know: if people can belong long enough to observe how God is alive among us, if people can belong long enough to see authentic love among us, if they can belong long enough to see whatever good exists in our lives as individuals and as a community, then they can come to belief."[27]

This is the kind of approach Ministry Marketing must take for postmodern people.

Practical application for Ministry Marketing to postmodern people

- Do some additional reading on Postmodernism.

See the Annotated Resource section for suggestions.

- Make it easy for not-as-yet-Christians to become involved with the church by hosting non-threatening, no-commitment-required activities.

Providing music, movies, and coffee discussion groups are one idea to start. Regarding music, that doesn't mean thirty minutes of praise choruses, which are great for the church service, but not necessarily for outreach events. It means the kind of music popular with your target audience—background music for coffee and conversational music.

- Market your message where not-as-yet-Christians will see it.

The church page of the Saturday edition of the local newspaper doesn't rate real high here. Few postmoderns cruise the church ads looking for the answers to life. Instead, think about placing an ad in the personals section. Or how about the sports page? Or the garage sales section? It may cost a bit more to advertise in these sections, but think how powerful an ad like this, listed in the garage sale section, could be:

"Ever feel your life resembles a pile of junk you'd sell cheaply? What if somebody told you that your life was of incredible worth? You are invited to coffee and music at OUR CHURCH BASEMENT CAFE to find out more."

- Advertising at the movie theater is another good idea.

Many theaters have local advertisements before the feature film. Your church could buy some of those minutes. Here is an ad idea from a woman who attended one of my seminars:

The screen is black as these words appear: "Are you here alone? Don't be alone forever. Come to [your church here]"

The woman who shared this ad idea with me commented, "Lots of people go to the movies alone. It was the perfect place for that kind of message."

Be sure to mention a specific event, with date and time included. Or advertise your church's web site (not the regular church site, but one designed by and for postmodern explorers of spirituality).

• Go fishing.

That's not a postmodern term, but initiate a direct mail marketing campaign to all the names of people in your county who have gotten divorced. This information is in the public record and can be found with a little research. Send a low-key, non-threatening invitation to the people on this list, inviting them to an event at your church for singles. Keep sending invitations for months, even if you don't get a response. The last chapter has a story about the results of a mailing like this.

• Create contemporary-looking ads for bus stops around town.

I know of a church that did that. The graphics were very stylized, using a contemporary-looking cross. The text said, "Jesus said He was the only way to God." Off-center and to the side, more text read, "What if He's right?" An invitation to a Saturday seeker service, with time and location listed, was in the lower right corner.

This last example is tricky. This kind of an ad, with its clear challenge to right and wrong and absolute answers, probably wouldn't appeal to a postmodern audience. But this church was located in a community whose residents weren't largely post-modern. It was an advertising campaign for that particular church and it was very successful.

Remember: Postmoderns make up only *part* of the church's Ministry Marketing audience. The next section discusses this fact in more detail.

Your Audience Is Diverse

You must do church differently for different cultures.

Today, many different cultures and subcultures can exist in the same community. This is

Postmodern thinking is important to understand, but not everyone fits that description. Some folks listen to FOX News; some listen to CNN. Some vote Republican; some vote Demo-crat. For some "the war" means the Civil War; to others it's Vietnam. Until you figure out which is which in your community, and unless you fit in and embrace the same mindset, your Ministry Marketing approach will probably be less than successful.

More important than reading theories or demographic statistics is reading your people. Find the Ministry Marketing approach that works for them. One of the things my constant travel has taught me is that the postmodern mindset is far more a result of geography and cultural setting than a characteristic of the current age. Labels break down when you talk to real people who are varied and orncry. Often, people don't fit easily into any one category.

especially true in urban settings. In Fort Lauderdale alone we have churches from many cultural backgrounds. Some of our churches are redneck; others are Old South in style and reach people from Alabama and Georgia. Some are blue collar; others target the up and out. Some are truly international in mix; others are Island back or Hispanic or Haitian. Some are bilingual.[28]

—Dan Southerland,
Transitioning: Leading Your Church through Change

Practical advice on Ministry Marketing for today's mixed mindsets

- When you engage someone in a spiritual conversation, find out his or her mindset. Don't assume you know the meaning of any religious terms he or she uses. Ask questions until you figure it out. Asking people what newspapers they read, their favorite TV shows and talk shows will give you an idea of their approach to the world.

- Learn about postmodernism and how to be a spiritual friend and a storyteller. Also, learn classic apologetics and how to argue truth with passion and patience. Some great modern resources in the apologetic area include books by Lee Strobel, especially the *Case for Christ* and *Case for Faith,* and resources by Hank Hanegraf. Other resources may be found on the web site for the Christian Research Institute, at www.equip.org.

- Have a full tool kit of approaches when it comes to helping people come closer to Jesus.

A good carpenter doesn't just use a hammer to build a house. Sometimes a drill is needed.

You'd best be handy with as many tools as you can master, so you can use the appropriate tool when it's needed.

- Find out what tools you are best at using and form or join a community with others who are good with other tools.

In *Contagious Christianity* (a great book, highly recommended), the authors have a list of the various ways people share their faith. Some are good with apologetics, some with hard-hitting, in-your-face evangelism, some with hospitality approaches. Be who you are and develop your tool set, but value the approaches of others and be sure your Ministry Marketing team uses a variety of approaches.

- This is very important—if you move to a new part of the country, or even to a different part of your state or town, take some time to determine the mindset of the people there before you attempt to do any kind of Ministry Marketing. Don't assume that the approaches you used in the past will work in a new area.

Diverse marketing with ethnic sensibilities in mind

Many churches today work in multicultural settings. Outreach that involves more than one cultural, language, or ethnic group has homework to do before it begins. An excellent book on marketing to various ethnic groups in America is *Designing Across Cultures* by Ronnie Lipton.[29]

The book describes in great detail how to market to the various ethnic cultures. Included are chapters on ministering to Hispanic Americans, African Americans, Asian American, and European Americans. The book starts by advising, "Begin by knowing enough about your audience to keep from offending it. Like the Hippocratic oath sworn by doctors: 'First do no harm.'"[30]

What is offensive? Some things that offend a particular group may surprise you, thus the need for carefully study. For example, the book cautions that for many Asians, white is the color associated with funerals. For Koreans, white and yellow are funeral colors, and chrysanthemums are funeral flowers. In both of these cultures, names of living persons should never be written in red ink because that symbolizes death.[31]

It helps to know these cultural sensibilities or you can make major marketing and communication errors unintentionally. For example, if you plan a fall banquet to help a Korean congregation in outreach, don't use yellow napkins with a white tablecloth and yellow or white mums as table decorations. If you plan a Valentine's Day outreach celebration and print the names of attendees for place cards, don't use red ink. All of these activities, though common and appropriate to the holidays for European Americans, would be insensitive and insulting to Korean Americans.

In communicating with an ethnic group, as with all groups, you want to do more than avoid the negatives. Learn how to build upon positive ethnic connotations in your communications as well. Lipon puts it this way, "If all you do is avoid offending, you'll miss the opportunity to connect. For that you have to look deeper."[32]

Ministry Marketing tips adapted from Designing Across Cultures[33]

- Observe your audience. In every area where there are large ethnic groups, they will have their own publications. Look at these publications for styles, colors, and ways of illustrating concepts.

- Include members of your target group in your ministry outreach team. Give them permission to tell you when you are offensive or off-track.

- Get advice for publications from the Internet. Research the audience. Get copies of publications produced by the group. Look for marketing research on your target group.

- Consider working with a consultant who interacts with your target group on a regular basis.

- Pray for sensitivity, humility, and the ability to see through eyes other than those of the culture of your birth.

SECTION TWO:

Characteristics of Easy Ministry Marketing

Many of the characteristics that ought to characterize our individual marketing pieces are a direct result of the shift in our audience. Though based on time-tested marketing wisdom, I've modified some of these recommendations to match the needs of contemporary audiences. For example, since people today tend to be indifferent (and sometimes honestly hostile) to authority, it has become even more important to be people-centered in all your marketing projects as we will discuss in the chapter on *Ministry Marketing Is People-Centered.*

Since people today are very time-starved, it is critical that our marketing is precise, complete, and gives all the information to audiences with no time to call back for more information or search for details, as is advised in the chapter on *Ministry Marketing Is Precise.*

Since people today are spiritually seeking, but often in nontraditional ways, our marketing communications may be far more effective if they are pop-culture savvy and the chapter on Pop Culture will give you lots of ideas to make those connections.

It was just before the Passover Feast. Jesus knew that the time had come for him to leave this world and go to the Father. Having loved his own who were in the world, he now showed them the full extent of his love . . . Jesus . . . got up from the meal, took off his outer clothing, and wrapped a towel around his waist. After that, he poured water into a basin and began to wash his disciples' feet . . . "Do you understand what I have done for you?" he asked them. "You call me 'Teacher' and 'Lord,' and rightly so, for that is what I am. Now that I, your Lord and Teacher, have washed your feet, you also should wash one another's feet."
—John 13:1-14, NIV

Finally, because your audience today is so diverse, one thing is good for everyone in marketing: joy. The chapter on *Playful* gives us ideas on how to incorporate joy into our work.

CHAPTER 6:

Easy Ministry Marketing Is People-Centered

Focus on the people you want to reach and not on yourself in your marketing projects. That seems obvious, doesn't it?

This rule, however, is routinely ignored in Ministry Marketing. Ministries ignore people by focusing more on what the ministry has to offer, as opposed to what people need. If you don't know the difference in focus and don't produce your marketing materials with the correct focus, you won't get the response you want. Let me give you an example of this from my experience.

> *You are not the customer . . . remember to secure the reader's attention first, then state the benefits of doing business with you, and finally tell exactly what action the reader must take—make a phone call, write a letter, read page five of the Sunday paper.*[34]
> —Jay Conrad Levinson, *Guerilla Marketing*

A number of years ago I was doing quite a bit of communication consulting in Colorado Springs. I mostly worked with Christian organizations, but a friend asked me if I'd work with the Consumer Credit Counseling group. Unlike many of the deceptive credit counseling groups that have appeared in the last number of years, this group genuinely helped people with financial problems. They helped people avoid bankruptcy and foreclosure, they held budget workshops, they did extensive financial counseling, and they worked out payment plans with creditors. They charged almost nothing for their services because they were almost totally underwritten by the United Way.

Their problem was a lack of clientele. They had a large office, staff, and extensive programs, but few clients. However, people in Colorado Springs greatly needed their help. That year *60 Minutes* did a program naming Colorado Springs the foreclosure capital of America.

In an effort to get people to come to them, the United Way paid to have a brochure created to market their services that was placed by the teller's window in banks all over the city. No one would pick the brochures up, and that's when they called me. I took one look at the brochure and identified the problem: the marketing communication was so focused on what the credit counseling group had to offer that it ignored the needs of the people it wanted to help.

How to determine what your audience really needs

Put yourself in the place of the person who needs your help. In this example, imagine you are terribly in debt. You are afraid you might lose your home. You know you've really messed up. While depositing a check at the bank, you look up and see a big, dark blue brochure from Consumer Credit Counseling. Huge white letters across the front say, "FREE HELP FOR PEOPLE WITH DEBT PROBLEMS."

Are you going to pick that up? I don't think so. To pick up that brochure in a public place is just like announcing to everyone, "Did you all notice? I have a debt problem, I'm a real loser."

When I saw the brochure, I told them, "Of course nobody is going to pick this up—you are publicly embarrassing potential clients!"

The folks at Consumer Credit Counseling felt so bad. They were genuinely caring people. They were telling people about what they had to offer when they advertised, "Free Help for People with Debt Problems." But what people needed before they could take advantage of that offer was to not be embarrassed in a public place before they could get help.

We brainstormed about a new slogan and someone in the group came up with this one: "DO YOU KNOW SOMEONE WHOSE BILLS ARE BIGGER THAN THEIR PAYCHECK?"

It was a great slogan. Picking up a brochure with that message on the cover doesn't necessarily mean that you're picking it up for yourself. You could be picking it up for Uncle Harry, who really has a problem with money.

We produced a brochure with that slogan on the cover. The new advertising campaign was a success and many people got help.

A Christian counseling center changes its approach

A local Christian counseling center had a similar problem—great services, but not very many people took advantage of them. This counseling center distributed its brochure in the lobbies of churches. It was a simple brochure that said, "FREE COUNSELING." This brochure didn't seem nearly as offensive as the one that shouted "Debt Problems!" but still, not many people picked it up. After I shared the story about the counseling center in a seminar I taught, a woman named Jan asked me to look at her brochure. I suggested that it could potentially be really embarrassing for people in church to admit they have any kind of problem that would require counseling help.

For example, as the head deacon's wife, even if you and your husband have had a rip-roaring fight on the way to church, you put on your church happy face for the service. On the way out of the service, you see the brochure announcing "Free Counseling," but you know that if you pick up that brochure then another church member will assume, "Amy and Joe are fighting again." So you don't pick it up and don't get help.

Jan's group wanted to help people, and after the seminar she went back to her office and redesigned a brochure that now had the slogan, "When someone you know is hurting, the Samaritan Counseling Center is here to help." Jan took the new brochure around to churches and a few months later I got a call from her.

"I thought you'd want to know," she reported. "In the first three months that we distributed the new brochure, we had to refill the racks more than we did in the entire previous year! We are getting so many more calls and helping lots more people!"

It might take some time and thought, but as the above examples illustrate, try to create Ministry Marketing that focuses on the needs of your people and not just a description of the help offered.

Practical applications for Ministry Marketing

Broadcast your message on the station people listen to. In secular marketing it is often said, "Everybody listens only to station WIFM." That's true. People evaluate everything by asking "Who's In It For Me?" At first that sounds selfish, but it really isn't. Nobody has time to listen to every program, attend every event, or read every piece of mail that he or she receives. We all have to screen what comes into our lives. We all have to ask, "What will help me, my family, my kids? What will meet my needs?" The Bible itself tells us we need to make the most of our time (Eph. 5:16).

You help people make the most of their time when you answer the question, "What's in it for me" in your staff meetings and clearly communicate the answer in your Ministry Marketing materials. For example, if you are offering a parenting seminar, don't advertise it as "Biblical Principles for Effective Parenting"—that's what you have to offer. Not everyone feels they need that, especially if they don't read the Bible. Instead market it in this way, "Sanity Savers for Stressed Parents." You could use exactly the same material, but come at it from the point of meeting needs. Make it the sort of event to which parents can bring their unchurched friends and they will look at the church as a place where problems are shared and solved.

Take some time to discover needs

If you don't know what people need in your church or community, ask them. In one church, a pastor challenged his staff to go out on the street and ask ten people what they considered were the greatest needs in their community. It was a beach community and a majority of people responded that the litter and trash on the beach really bothered them. In response, the church decided to sponsor a beach clean-up day every month as a way of serving their community in the name of Jesus. If you do something like this, wear bright-colored t-shirts with the name of the church on them and have business card invitations to your church ready to give to folks who ask what you are doing.

Sometimes the need is obvious and action is required

Sometimes you don't need to take a survey to determine needs in your community. A pastor in one of my seminars told me about the outreach ministry of a church outside the Washington D.C. area during the time of the sniper shootings. Several people had been randomly killed at gas stations in the area, and weeks went by without the police finding the shooters. During that time the church stationed teams of volunteers at various gas stations. They wore vests that identified them as being from the church and carried business cards that they gave to people who asked about the church. As people drove up to the gas station, the church volunteers offered to pump the gas. They offered to take the place of a stranger and risked being the next target of a sniper attack.

We don't often face situations like the sniper incidents, but in every community there are needs and community chores no one wants to do. If church groups do those things in the name of Jesus, it will be some of the best Ministry Marketing imaginable.

CHAPTER 7:

Easy Ministry Marketing Is Pop Culture Savvy

For a missionary to go to any foreign mission the preparation is extensive. Missionaries study the culture, learn the language, and speak with previous missionaries who have gone before them, mining them for wisdom and advice. To be a missionary to our communities today, we

The new global superpower is entertainment.[35]
—Craig Detweiler and Barry Taylor, *a matrix of meaning*

need to look outside the church doors and learn the culture of the people we want to reach and relate to with our Ministry Marketing materials.

Understanding the culture of unchurched people today is even more important than in the past because, as stated earlier, most people do not share with us a collective church consciousness. Church attendance by the community and biblical literacy through out the community does not provide us with shared stories as it did in the past.

Today popular culture provides a base for shared stories between the church and people outside of the church. Craig Detweiler and Barry Taylor in *a matrix of meanings: finding God in pop culture* (the title is in lower case) state, "Like the Old Testament writings, pop culture is the collected wisdom of our era."[36]

The book gives abundant examples of today's culture and how people use it in their search for God through advertising, music, fashion, art, celebrity, movies, television, and sports. This book is highly recommended reading for insights as to how popular culture talks about spirituality. If you read *a matrix of meanings*, ask the Holy Spirit to give you eyes to see beyond what might be shocking content for some members of your church, and instead see into the hearts of the people who need to receive your Ministry Marketing.

Let the book reveal to you the questions asked by today's culture. The book can provide hundreds of ideas for bridge activities and approaches between the church and not-as-yet Christians.

Another useful book is *Christianity Explored*. It explains how to share the Christian story with people outside the church, and the style in which it is written is an example of how to use pop culture to explain spiritual truths. The authors, Rico Tice and Barry Cooper, use movies, sports, and celebrity quotations to illustrate spiritual truths. For example, early in the book they talk about connecting with unchurched people this way:

> One other factor that has led some people to feel that God exists is the human sense of loneliness, emptiness and restlessness, not to mention our sense of the infinite. That's why the background story of The Matrix is so ingenious: it feels like it might be true. In the film, Morpheus tells Neo: 'Let me tell you why you are here. It's because you know something. What you know you can't explain but you feel it. You've felt it your entire life. There is something wrong with the world. You don't know what it is, but it's there, like a splinter in your mind driving you mad.'[37]

To prove God's existence and to show that sin separates us from God is a difficult and challenging place to start sharing the gospel story. Using *The Matrix* as an analogy works well because many people have seen the movie and know what it feels like to have "a splinter in your mind." People can relate to the presence of an uneasy feeling, just below the level of conscious thought, that at our core something is not right between our Creator and us. *The Matrix* can be a bridge to a discussion of spiritual issues. This is just one example of how the book uses pop culture as a bridge to sharing the gospel.

Practical suggestions for pop culture savvy Ministry Marketing

- **Read *a matrix of meaning* and discuss it as a staff.** It can be a somewhat lengthy, intimidating book. Assign staff members to read various chapters and report what they find to the rest of the staff to make it more manageable.

- **Read *Christianity Explored.*** Look for ways that this book uses pop culture as a bridge to share the gospel message. Discuss how you might use similar approaches.

Using these books as inspiration, brainstorm additional ways you can use pop culture to market your ministry and share the gospel message.

- **Regularly visit http://www.hollywoodjesus.com.** Sign up for the e-mail newsletter list. This is a wonderful site and resource if you want to keep up with pop culture, particularly as it pertains to movies and media. It has movie reviews written by Christians that discuss topics beyond how many times profanity was used in a movie and how often sex or violence was portrayed. The reviews vary in approach and quality, as they are written by a large number of contributors, but all are useful. There are also great ideas on how to use movies as outreach events. The links from the site are priceless. David Bruce, the creator of the site, is an extraordinary example of someone with a heart for integrating the gospel into pop culture and the practical savvy on how to do it in our world. If you get a chance to hear him speak in person, go.

- **Go to movies, particularly the popular ones.** Watch TV in order to pick up on analogies you can use in your Ministry Marketing messages. You do not have to violate personal moral standards to do this. Go to movies you are comfortable attending. If you work with GenX college students, you will probably be comfortable attending movies that may not work for those working with grade school kids and parents. You can find connections with your target audience from all sorts of movies. The American Tract Society (www. atstracts.org) does this with a wonderful gospel tract based on the animated movie *Finding Nemo*, entitled "Finding Your Way Home." It's a great example of how a movie may be used as a bridge to

Ministry Marketing the gospel message. Check out the American Tract Society web site for well-done, movie-related gospel tracts whenever major movies are released. The movie doesn't have to be "R" rated to communicate a profound message.

- **Read USA TODAY, your local paper, and magazines enjoyed by your target audience.** Try adapting some ideas from the stories you find. For example, USA TODAY and other newspapers have run articles on speed dating. It's where folks sign up for a short coffee time with another person and then move to a different table with a new person. This is an excellent idea for a singles group. What if your church sponsored a version of it?

Use pop culture as a goldmine of great ideas to help you reach your world and not as simply an expression of the current depravity of humanity to be avoided at all costs.

CHAPTER 8:

The Foundation for Ministry Marketing Made Easy

We are all familiar with the principle stated in Luke 16:10. This principle is also a key characteristic to remember in your Ministry Marketing when you want people to respond.

> *"He that is faithful in that which is least, is faithful also in much."*
> —Luke 16:10 (KJV)

As I have stated, one of the occupational hazards of Ministry Marketing is becoming overly familiar with events. It is easy to assume that everyone knows the people, time, and location associated with events, but they don't. When we become overly familiar with the details of the events we are advertising, and if Ministry Marketing pieces (either on the web, on PowerPoint®, in print, or communicated verbally) don't give complete information about where an event is to take place, the time it is to start and end, and whether or not childcare is to be provided, then don't be surprised if the response is not what you expect. Complete, pertinent details must be included in every piece.

Regular attendees at your church are too busy to call the church office in order to confirm basic details. Newcomers feel like everybody else knows who is in charge or where an event is to be held, and they may be too shy or embarrassed to ask.

Repeat the details for every new reader

A key principle for all direct mail marketing (and one that is good to remember in any kind of marketing) is that even though a certain marketing piece might be repeated ten times, the tenth time may be the first time that any particular individual sees it or pays attention to it. Therefore, include key information *every time*. Though the details that need to be included seem obvious to you, my experience with evaluating thousands of publications has taught me they aren't. The following are some of the key items to include.

Clearly describe the event

If the event's name doesn't clearly describe what is going on, clarify it. For example, my church had an event known as "Hospitality Night." From the title alone no one would automatically know that this event was a free meal and game night for singles, hosted by married couples in the church.

Unless it is totally self-explanatory, explain in your marketing pieces what an event is.

We now call this event "Singles' Games & Goodies Night" and many more people come because they know what is going on.

In the church we have all kinds of cute names that don't make any sense at all to the people not already involved in the program or activity. You must make names clearly describe events if you want new people to attend. Be especially careful of acronyms, and always spell out the name if you use them.

For example: our singles ministry was called OASIS. In all of our publications, I had a rule that the acronym name was never to be used alone because alone it didn't make sense.

What's an oasis? It is a word used for all sorts of things from bars, to a brand of bottled water, to a place for camels to drink in the desert. When we use the name OASIS in publications for church, it always says, "OASIS, single adult ministry." It is a simple addition. We kept our name, but the publication material always communicate what the group is about.

Make this a rule to use any time a group or event has an acronym for a name. OASIS stood for Our Adult Singles in Service: Service to God, Service to Others, Service to Our World. We don't have to say all of that every time, and you don't need to explain in detail the meaning of every acronym, but give people a clear idea of what it stands for. The simple way to insure this happens is to establish a publication guideline in your church that whenever an acronym, or any name that is not self-explanatory, is used it is followed by a comma and a brief description of the group. For example:

- OASIS, single adult ministry
- Becomers, new Christian class
- SAM, senior adult ministry
- COPS, church office professionals

When you do this you keep everyone's favorite name (that the regular attenders can use) but it also provides a description for newcomers and visitors.

Location

Give the address, and if necessary, directions to events. A good way to do this is to give directions to events starting from the church. Most everyone knows where the church is since that is where he or she heard about the event. Especially in a large metropolitan area, a common starting point such as the church is helpful.

Be careful about downloading maps from Mapquest and similar web sites. These maps are almost always impossible to read when printed. The printed directions from these sites are much more useful. In addition, be careful to physically check out any directions downloaded from the Internet because they are often not entirely accurate. More than once I've found a left turn recommended when a right turn was the correct one.

Contact person

No matter how well known you believe event leaders are in your church, most folks have no idea whether it's Cathy, Jane, or Pastor Andy who is the contact person for a specific event. Always give the name, and if appropriate, the ministry title for the person, such as "youth director" or "children's choir director." This is especially important for any event that involves children or teens. Parents need a contact person so they will know who is in charge.

Phone numbers, e-mail address, and miscellaneous contact information

We have come to expect instant access to people, and contact information needs to be provided in event communications. A contact phone number for every event, activity, and ministry opportunity is essential. Including the phrase, "Call the church office for more information," is not the best approach. It is overwhelming for office staff or pastors to be solely responsible for providing details for every church event.

Sometimes, churches make use of telephone voicemail, which is even worse, because callers often need answers to questions immediately. Make it a rule that the person on the staff or a volunteer who is in charge of the event is also responsible to receive phone calls about it. Provide both a primary and alternative phone number. If people are asked to call the church, be sure to include a direct number or an extension that can be dialed directly. Also provide an e-mail address for people who prefer to ask for and receive information using the Internet, Blackberry, or web-enabled phone.

The church telephone Ministry Marketing sabotage

Many businesses today have someone answering the phone twenty-four hours a day, seven days a week. This is not realistic for most churches. However, one of the biggest Ministry Marketing mistakes that a church can make is not to have someone answer the phone during the church's prime operational hours, including evenings, weekends, and on Sundays.

Not doing so is a marketing disaster. Can you imagine a movie theater closing down the box office and shutting off the phones on the weekends and expecting people to come to the movies? Can you imagine a business at the mall with no one at the cash register at night because they'd already worked during the day and wanted to go home?

We know that would mean death to any business, but similar actions are common practice for churches. Often, churches create vague invitations with nonspecific directions to church events. When people come to the church building in the evenings, nobody is in the "Welcome Center" to tell them where the singles or youth group is conducting their "Outreach Event." Then they are surprised no outsiders show up for their events.

Suggestions for dealing with information blackouts at your church

Like everything else in Ministry Marketing, be motivated by the Great Commission (that the eternal destiny of souls really is at stake), and by the Great Commandment (the mandate to express the love of Jesus to others). Here are some ideas of what you might do to help individuals who seek information about events at your church:

- **Form a communications team that is responsible for covering the phones.** This can be a little or a big team, but realize that comprehensive telephone coverage is too difficult and time-consuming for one person.

- **Cover as many hours as possible.** Consider using call forwarding during church off-hours, and ask members of your team to take turns answering church information questions. Some people in your church may do shift work and would be willing to take calls at odd times.

- **Be sure you train phone volunteers.** Answering questions about the church is similar to working a crisis phone hot line—phone volunteers need to know which questions to answer and which ones to refer.

- **Whenever your church hosts an event at night, be sure the lights are on and that someone is out front welcoming people.** Be sure your signs can be seen at night and the parking lot is well lit and safe. If an event is in the basement or room near the back of the church be sure there are directional signs leading the way.

- **Have someone in the Welcome Center as much as possible whenever any event is going on at the church.** For the night of their Christmas Eve Candlelight service, one church had its Welcome and Church Information Center closed. Not only did they miss out on marketing opportunities, but this was also an area that had a solid, heavy metal door that came down over the opening. It was located right as people came into the church and looked very uninviting. The church did not come across as a place where a visitor would want to return.

- **Whenever possible, make sure the person in charge of an event has a cell phone** (switch the phone to silent as the event begins). Sometimes people hear about things at the last minute and their first reaction is to make a phone call to see if it is OK to attend. Receiving and responding to that call is important.

- **How do other businesses in your community make themselves available 24/7?** Different communities will have different expectations and levels of service. Don't allow your church to be the worst entity in town when it comes to responding to the needs of potential members.

Time and duration

Providing the start time of events is a crucial piece of information, but the start time is often left out of pieces because planners assume that, "Everybody knows when the newcomer coffee starts." Everybody doesn't know.

Just as important as the start time, an event's duration and ending time should also be provided. Parents who have made childcare arrangements and parents of children and youth who transport their children to events need to know when the event will end. Newcomers need to know if they are committing to an hour or an entire evening. For people who are juggling busy schedules, the duration of an event can be a major determinate in committing to attend. Always have both start and ending times listed.

Cost or contribution required

If a person shows up to an event and can't pay for it, he or she may turn around and walk away. If there is no cost, let people know. If food is a part of the event, but participants have the option of bringing food from home to share, state that. No matter what the plan, be sure that the person at the door has the grace and kindness to welcome everyone, regardless.

If a scholarship is available for events that require a fee, state it clearly in your marketing and tell readers the specific name of the contact person. If a person needs to make use of the scholarship, it will embarrass him or her to call the church without knowing whom he or she needs to talk to. Whenever people have to ask for money, or are setting up a counseling appointment, or any other potentially difficult communication, be certain to provide a direct number or extension, if possible.

Little things mean a lot in Ministry Marketing communications

It isn't easy to include these smaller details in communication, but the little things are essential if you want people to respond to your Ministry Marketing messages. When it seems like a chore to track down and include details for events, remember that you are engaging in servant work. Think of it as foot washing with the computer. Many Ministry Marketing jobs are repetitive and boring. Remind yourself that the details you provide may be just the bit of information a person needs to get him or her to an event where he or she will meet Jesus.

CHAPTER 9:

Easy Ministry Marketing Is Playful

Much Ministry Marketing is often so deadly serious. We tend to present a God that is no fun at all. That *is* a problem.

We serve a Lord who started out His ministry doing a lot of picnics and fish fries. And, there was that incident at the wedding. Can you imagine, those huge water containers full of wine? Today it would be like filling a hot tub with the very best vintage you could imagine.

In a recent episode of the television program, Joan of Arcadia, *God tells Joan to throw a party. Joan snaps back, "I didn't think you were into that."*

"That's the problem," God replies.

Strong or weak, however you interpret the condition of the wine, that was a pretty playful way to start a ministry.

The Bible tells us, " . . . the common people heard [Jesus] gladly" (Mark 12:37, KJV). *The Message* paraphrases Mark 12:37 as, "The large crowd was delighted with what they heard." The crowds spoken of here weren't religious audiences. Today, it would more likely be the folks who watch MTV and the Comedy Channel than the folks who watch TBN.

The crowds clearly loved Jesus. The scriptural image of Jesus as fun is so different from the way the church often portrays him.

Practical ideas to make your Ministry Marketing playful

These are all stories shared with me by people who have attended my seminars. Use them to inspire you to do some fun things in your Ministry Marketing:

- Give people balloons, lots of balloons. Give balloons to kids who visit Sunday School classes, and as invitations to children's events. Most any specialty shop can print your message on balloons. One church gave everyone a helium balloon on Easter Sunday. The congregation then went outside and released the balloons to celebrate the resurrection of Jesus.

• A single adult ministry group handed out free ice-cream bars in the park on a hot day. Little cards were attached that said, "People say nothing is free in life, but this is. Enjoy! And know God's love is free also. If you want to hear more about it, visit us some time at [Name of Your Church]."

• A church in Texas repeatedly held one major outreach event—a car wash. They called it an extra-special, we-almost-detail-your-car, car wash. It was free. Every person in the car received a free Texas BBQ sandwich and a free soda while the car was washed. The volunteers who washed the cars are what made this event really fun. It wasn't just teenagers. It was church members of all ages, including the senior pastor and staff. The church grew from eighteen to 2,300 in a few years. I imagine I'd visit a church if the pastor washed my car and gave me a free sandwich and soda pop.

• In a church where people normally took their event announcements quite seriously and ignored most of them, one innovative secretary tore the edges off of important announcements and scattered them on the floor of the church. She said, "If it looks like trash, folks will probably pick it up and read it." It worked.

• A church secretary decided that the only time people sit still to read what is going on in the church is in the bathroom. So she had Plexiglas newspaper holders installed in the ladies bathroom stalls and over the men's urinals. She created a publication called "THE STALL STREET JOURNAL." The paper advertised upcoming church events and attendance increased.

• Another group printed big notices backwards and posted them on the wall across from bathroom mirrors. When people look up while combing their hair, they read the notices.

- For an abundance of wonderful, fun, fantastic ideas, go to http://www.servantevangelism.com. Steve Sjogren and others have books, resources, a conference, and a section entitled "Planned Acts of Christian Kindness" that will give you hundreds of fun and effective ways to make your Ministry Marketing fun and effective. My web site also contains a current listing of the fun Ministry Marketing ideas I hear about from people who take my seminars.

Consider firing the coffee police

The coffee police are the people who stand at the door of the sanctuary of churches and forbid anyone to enter with a cup of coffee. Because of them, the following scenario happens far too often.

Picture a church that has a great coffee cart on the patio outside. They make real lattes (and charge for them) and offer great muffins. A visitor dashes up late, having had no breakfast, sees the coffee and muffins and thinks, "Wow, what a great place!" The visitor purchases a latte and muffin and approaches the door, thinking he or she might really enjoy this church thing.

The contented visitor is abruptly stopped.

"You can't bring that inside!" the coffee police informs the visitor.

"What? I just paid three dollars for this!"

"I'm sorry, we have to be careful of the carpet. This is God's house, you know," the coffee police replies.

The contented visitor is now a very grumpy visitor. Most likely the visitor will leave, choosing to keep the coffee and muffin rather than discard them to go in and sing songs that he or she doesn't know.

Coffee or carpets—a Ministry Marketing dilemma

If people really are the most important thing to your church, then they are more important than the condition of the carpet. On the other hand, if your church cares that much about the sanctuary carpet, don't offer people coffee. An alternative is to provide bottled water.

A customized label with the church's logo can even be printed on the bottle. It is better, however, to offer nothing to drink than to put people in an adversarial situation by giving them something and not allowing them to drink it inside the church sanctuary.

Coffee is a big deal in our culture today. I admit to a serious Starbucks addiction (grande nonfat latte is my drink of choice). Aside from my addiction, there is a significant marketing reason why there are coffee places in airports, grocery stores, and bookstores today. People really like to drink coffee. In addition, somehow clutching a cup of coffee forms a shield against insecurity. Coffee gives some people courage to meet others, face new situations, and sip on something rather than talk.

People show up at work, movies, airplanes (you can't take a Swiss Army knife or a laser pointer on airplanes, but nobody turns away coffee), and numerous other places clutching their $3.85 latte from Starbucks. Why is church the only place you can't bring your Starbucks?

A coffee cart with great coffee (sales can even help finance a mission)[38] is a wonderful way to welcome people. Nineteenth-century Gothic cathedrals may have legitimate architectural issues about not allowing coffee in the sanctuary. But for most churches, allowing people to bring coffee into the sanctuary is a legitimate, meaningful outreach action and great Ministry Marketing.

So what if the carpet has to be cleaned every week? What difference does it make if people have to come in and clean up trash after every service? Movie theaters do it all the time. What's the price of salvation? Most people aren't really that messy, anyway. Even if they are, remember sheep are messy, too. Shepherds are supposed to pick up after the sheep, and shepherds don't give sheep lectures on how they ought to eat or drink.

Sometimes earthly ministry is so serious, but it won't always be that way

People sometimes talk about how they look forward to having their questions answered when they get to heaven. I've always felt that most of the questions won't matter once we get there.

But I do have one request: I want to hear Jesus laugh.

SECTION THREE:

Key Ministry Marketing Publications

In sections one and two we established a foundation for Ministry Marketing, gained an understanding of the target audience, and identified characteristics that are helpful to remember in Marketing Ministry. Now is the time to apply this knowledge in order to create marketing projects that touch people with the gospel story.

> *"That part of the line,"* *he said, "where I thought* *I could serve best was* *also the part that seemed* *to be thinnest. And to it I* *naturally went."*[39]
> —C. S. Lewis, *God in the Dock*

In the words of Lewis, I have found the line "to be thinnest" in regard to the production of ordinary Ministry Marketing pieces. Many of the books that I have read on marketing in the church seem to be long on demographics, statistics, and studies but the advice is quite thin on how to actually connect with the people you meet at the grocery store and want to invite to church. Great theory abounds, but not much exists on what needs to be produced in the church office next week that will get people from Sunday morning service into small groups.

This section will fortify that section of the line. In it you'll get practical advice on what might be termed "front-line" or "first-contact" marketing pieces. You'll learn what to include on invitation cards, postcards, church bulletins, bulletin inserts, and niche newsletters.

These publications are truly what make up the first critical contact of Ministry Marketing in our world. They literally touch people, get them to attend events, and bring them back to church. Unless you do these well, you may not get a chance to do anything else with your intended audience. It's hard to share your story using multi-media, seeker-friendly, fantastic music, drama, and a carefully crafted, need-oriented sermon if your neighborhood people never set foot inside your church.

Invitation cards and postcards can get them there, your bulletin and bulletin inserts will get them to come back, and your niche newsletter can involve them on a continuing basis.

Of course, there are many more publications, media, and methods that can be used in marketing (in my seminars we spend a day discussing quite a few of them). But every book has its limits and given the size constraints and introductory nature of this one, I felt these were the most important to discuss.

CHAPTER 10:

Business, Invitation Cards, and Postcards

If you want your church to grow, invite everyone in the church to take part in the adventure of Ministry Marketing. The Great Commission is commanded for every Christian. It isn't only part of the job description for the paid clergy. We are all commanded to share the gospel story.

Most people in the church are not involved in evangelism. One reason they aren't involved is because many people think that evangelism means going up to a total stranger and asking that person, "Are you saved?" Then, no matter what the answer, the belief is that we're supposed to recite a prepackaged presentation. Most folks won't, or can't, do that. It's scary, embarrassing, and often it isn't very effective. How can average folks share their faith?

> *Herein lies a fascinating paradox for direct marketers: the more sophisticated our futuristic database technology becomes, the more it allows us to treat customers just as individually as the corner merchant did generations ago.*[40]
> —Susan K. Jones,
>   *Creative Strategy in Direct Marketing*

Business and invitation cards

Business and invitation cards are two tremendously powerful tools that can "equip the saints to do the work of the ministry" (Eph. 5:12).

Imagine standing in line in the grocery story. The person in front of you picks up a tabloid and says something like, "You know, our world is really a scary place. I'm afraid to even get out of bed in the morning."

You might reply, "I agree. Our world is scary today. But our pastor is preaching a sermon this Sunday on "How to Have Peace in an Unpeaceful World." Why don't you come?" Chances are the person might respond by saying, "I'd really like to do that."

At this point one of two things can happen:

Option #1   Tell the person the name and location of your church. The person thanks you and leaves with the best of intentions, planning to show up on Sunday. However, Sunday arrives and he or she really wants to attend the church, but can't remember exactly where it is, or the exact name of the church, or what time the service starts. "I really hope I run into that nice person from the grocery store again," the person thinks. Of course, that doesn't happen, and the person stays home that Sunday and maybe every Sunday.

Option #2   Imagine the same conversation in the grocery store line, but after inviting the person to church, you pull out a business card to give the person. The business card is really an invitation card. Printed on the front it reads, "Welcome, Be Our Guest!" On the back of the card the person finds the name and address of the church, a contact phone number, web site address, map of location, and service times of your church.

"Here is a card about our church," you say. "It has our address and service times on Sunday, as well as times for some programs during the week. If you want to, check out our web site and find out a little more about us. As you can see, we have childcare for all of our services."

The person then leaves with concrete information about your church. Chances are he or she will check it out. Having a card like this turns a chance conversation into a potentially significant step on someone's spiritual journey.

Great for the church and for ministries in the church

In addition to creating cards such as this for the general church, a business card-size invitation card can be very useful for specialized ministries.

For example, one woman's passion for ministry was to encourage and reach out to young stay-at-home moms. She started a ministry at her church for them, but had trouble getting young moms to attend. Her kids were grown and she honestly didn't know anyone personally who fit into the group she wanted to reach. Attendance at her ministry meetings averaged about eight people, with over half of them the leaders.

After attending one of my seminars and hearing about the idea of invitation cards, I spoke with her and she decided to give them a try. She showed me a colorful, upbeat card and then shared her strategy with me.

"Here's what we do," she said, bubbling over with excitement. "Our ladies hang out in parks where moms take their kids. They scout out grocery and other stores during the times moms go shopping with their kids and they get into the longest lines behind mothers with children. They are intentional about starting up conversations with mothers and always pass on our invitation card. We now have over eighty young moms in our program!"

Tips for Ministry Business/Invitation cards

- Create invitation cards for your church as a whole, and specialized cards for large Sunday School classes, small groups, and specialized ministries in the church such as invitation cards for singles, recovery groups, MOPS, etc.

- In order to be effective, the cards do not have to be fancy, full-color, and professionally printed. They can be if you want them to be, but that is not essential for their use and success. A young mom who needs an occasional break from her kids doesn't care about the typeface or graphics of an invitational card. It will thrill her to find out about a free morning where her kids are safe while she meets with other mothers and receives encouragement.

- The basic information is most important. Be sure it is complete. Also, provide enough cards (hundreds, perhaps thousands) so that every person in your church or ministry can give them out continuously. Encourage people to carry business/invitation cards with them everywhere they go and give them out with enthusiasm and prayer.

The all-important postcard

While it may be true that there is no perfect marketing or communication piece, postcards come closest to perfection of any printed piece put out by churches today. Postcards are incredibly powerful and can be used for almost any marketing or communication message.

Direct mail marketing has used postcards extensively in the last few years because postcards are effective. People are so busy that they often don't take time to open and read messages arriving in sealed envelopes. As you go through your own mail this week, be conscious of how many unopened envelopes you toss into the trash. Compare what you do with unopened envelopes to what you do with the postcards you receive.

In addition to being easier to read, if the postcard announces an event you don't want to miss, or describes something you want to make certain your children attend, that postcard will end up on what I call communication central for every home—the refrigerator. If a message is on the refrigerator, there is a good chance action will be taken. If the event announcement languishes unread in an unopened envelope, it is as if the event never happened.

Postcard concerns and solutions

Many churches know that the use of postcards is a great marketing tool, but there are some major concerns that prevent their being used frequently, particularly for overall Ministry Marketing. Three of the top concerns are:

- the difficulty of balancing mail costs with the number of positive responses,
- the cost, either of creating or buying the postcards,
- the cost of postage and the difficulty of mailing in bulk.[41]

The following idea can be used for churches that cannot afford professionally created direct mail programs. It also works for churches that create a large volume of direct mailings that mix professionally created pieces with pieces they create themselves.

Postcard publicity and congregational involvement

A church secretary from a large church in Texas shared this great postcard publicity idea with me. She worked at a growing church of around 2,300 members. Her church used postcards to advertise many of its outreach events. She reported fantastic results with very little cost to the church, and the church frequently sent out huge mailings. This is how they did it:

- The church office staff designed and created a postcard advertising the event. It was attractive, but not terribly complex.

- The postcard was inexpensively printed on cardstock, with black typeface and an accent color using the church's RISO Digital Duplicator. The church printed thousands of cards fairly quickly with the RISO because they used 8½ x by 11 cardstock that was then power cut into four pieces.

- On Sunday morning, every person who attended worship was given five postcards in his or her bulletin.

- During the announcement time, the pastor stood up and said, "As you can see, all of you have five postcards in your bulletin for the upcoming Harvest Festival we'll be hosting at the church. Think of and pray for five friends whom you can invite. Address the postcard to them and please add a personal note. Please provide the stamps for your postcards. Additional cards are available in the back if you want to hand them out as invitations."

Why this plan works

- First, instead of an impersonal mailing list, the people that received this card were a marketer's dream. The list consisted of people who were personally known by the person inviting them. Additionally, a personal note encouraged them to attend.

- Second, asking everyone to provide his or her own stamps in a church of more than 2,000 (with each person asked to send out five cards) saved the church a tremendous amount of money.

- Finally, since each person addressed, stamped, and mailed his or her own cards, it saved the church a huge amount of work. Prayer can go along with each attached stamp.

Using this method, the church was able to do numerous large-scale mailing campaigns during the year with very little cost in time and money for the church staff. These mailings had a tremendous impact on the community.

Other benefits and variations

- Once again, the church in this instance equipped the saints to do the work of the ministry. People in the church became participants in the outreach efforts of the church, instead of expecting the staff to do it all.

- When people responded, they responded to a personal invitation. There was someone who prayed for them and who was there to greet them and make them feel welcome.

- This same method can be used for individual ministries in the church, such as the youth program, single adult ministry, and other small group recruitment efforts. In almost every area of ministry the leaders can make up postcards, reproduce them, and have members use them as invitations to be mailed or hand-delivered.

CHAPTER 11:

The Church Bulletin and Insert

The church bulletin is so important because for many people today, the church bulletin might be the first piece of Christian literature they see. If people do not grow up in church they won't encounter Christian literature in school, and they won't come across a gospel

> *The church bulletin is the most important piece of Christian literature printed today, outside the Bible.*
> —Yvon Prehn

message clearly presented in the media. Yet people have hungry hearts. They want to connect with their Creator and they come to our churches. We hand them the bulletin, but what does it say?

Sometimes it gives them the order of service and sometimes it doesn't. So they may or may not have any idea what is going on. It's often full of church terms like *introit*, *invocation*, *petitions* and *tithes*. The terms are seldom explained. It talks about the meetings of the AWANAS, the Growing Edge, and the Going Concern. It reminds people that the budget is $2,000 behind and they need to get their pledge cards in this week. It announces the "Adult Bible Study at the Johnsons—same time, same place!"

Instead of answering their spiritual questions, it often says to visitors, "this is an insider group and you don't belong here."

Suggestions for changes to the church bulletin

I'd love to see a revolution in church bulletins through the creation of wild, wonderful, seeker-friendly publications that welcome the stranger and affirm the regular attendee. But if your church isn't ready to take such a big step, I highly recommend the following changes:

Tell people what is going on: include an order of service

Not including an order of service is one of the most disturbing trends I see in many church bulletins today and this practice seems to be growing. So often I see bulletins that are simply collections of announcements with no mention at all of what will go on during the Sunday morning service.

We need to reverse this trend, because nothing about a Sunday morning church service is obvious to a visitor. Mark Mittelberg, in *Building a Contagious Church,* reminds us that visiting a church for the first time is like a visit to a Buddhist temple would be for most Christians.[42] Would you have any idea what to do? Would you know what is going to happen? Would you know how you are supposed to react? The bulletin must answer these questions for newcomers in your church and the order of service is the place to start.

How to tell them

In analyzing hundreds of bulletins, many middle-of-the-road, mainline denominations have a fairly clear order of service. The churches that seem to most often forgo an order of service and therefore confuse many visitors are the contemporary, charismatic churches, or the highly liturgical traditional churches. In contrast to this trend, I have come across a couple of exceptions that do a great job of explaining the order of service to unchurched visitors and they are described here.

An order of service for a contemporary church

What follows is from a church bulletin for a contemporary, charismatic church. The worship planners didn't assume that folks knew anything about what would happen in the service, and they explained it in this way:

> ***Our Worship Service:*** *Thanks for joining us today! We will begin with about thirty to forty minutes of singing. Feel free to sit, stand, sing, dance, or just listen as we express our worship to God using all of our heart, mind, soul, and body. If you don't know the songs, hang on, we'll sing them a couple of times—and don't worry, we didn't know them at first, either.*

The Message: A time of practical teaching from the Bible.

The Offering: This is a time for church members to share with the church financially. It is a way to thank God for God's blessings. If you are a visitor, don't feel you have to contribute—the only gift we'd like from you is your Connection Card. Consider this service our gift to you!

Prayer Time: There will be people up front after the service to pray for any needs you may have. Please come up if interested!

Refreshments: Join us for coffee, lemonade, and munchies in the lobby after the service.

This order of worship isn't complex or fancy, but by reading it a stranger would know what to do and wouldn't feel awkward.

Explanations in a liturgical bulletin

High liturgical styles of worship have their own challenges. Though many churches that worship in this style indicate an order of worship in the bulletin, a person who did not grow up in the tradition may not have any idea of the meaning of what they are reciting.

In order to help visitors feel welcome, some churches provide a running commentary down the left-hand margin of the bulletin that explains what is happening. In the example below, the bulletin had the traditional headings of *Invocation, Confession, Absolution,* and *Introit of the Day.* To the left of each of these sections were the following explanations:

"**Invocation**" means "calling on" and here we call on the Lord's presence.

In the "**Confession**" we name our sins silently before the Lord and accept responsibility for the harm they have caused in our relationships with God and each other.

111

> In the **"Absolution"** the Lord speaks through the office of pastor to apply to us the forgiveness Jesus won for us on the cross in a personal and public way (John 20:23).
>
> **"Introit"** means "entrance" in Latin. Now that we have been washed clean of our sins the pastor enters into the altar area. The Introit usually comes from a Psalm.

This bulletin's order of service continues in this way, providing excellent help to visitors who need explanations to help them understand what is happening in worship. Every church has terms that may not be familiar to visitors. Taking time to explain these words will do more to market your church positively than an expensive billboard on the freeway.

More ways to make the rest of the bulletin visitor friendly

Welcome people

It is amazing how few bulletins actually begin with a welcome! Welcome everyone before the order of service. It can be a long or short word of welcome, but it should be genuine and reflect the tradition of your church. A welcome on the second page or on the back of the bulletin (as is often the case) doesn't make sense.

Acknowledge both visitors and members in the announcement section

Some of the best bulletins actually have sections that say, "Welcome to Our Visitors" and then provide essential details, such as the location of the bathrooms, nursery, information table, etc. Also, these bulletins often invite folks for coffee after the service where they can meet people and ask questions.

In some of the same bulletins there is often a section entitled "Church News." Content like this accommodates visitors and people who don't know every detail of every event. The issue can be addressed this way: "Below are the various events hosted by our church in the coming weeks. Everyone is invited to these activities and we hope you'll attend. If you need more information or have questions, please call the contact numbers listed with each activity."

Don't list events that are closed to newcomers

I'll never forget a bulletin that contained a lengthy list of groups that met in one particular church, but provided no contact information. I pointed this out to the woman who put the bulletin together, stating that the contact information was missing. New folks, who might want to be part of the groups, wouldn't know who to call for information. The woman replied, "Oh, we don't do that—these are all closed groups and they don't want new members."

That isn't nice. Don't do that. If for some reason a group must be closed, then do not list it in the bulletin at all.

Include the Five Ws: who, what, when, where, and why

I think it could revolutionize churches if complete information about events was provided church bulletins.

The church staff works so hard to put together programs only to have bulletins leave out vital information. Always include who is putting on the program, what is going on, where it is being held, what time it starts and ends, the cost, and if child care is provided. If you leave out the "Five Ws" you will get a much smaller turnout than you want.

It is also important to repeat this information for several weeks if you expect people to respond. Remember, no one will see the bulletin as many times as you do. Because of work and school obligations, many members cannot attend every week.

Create a form for people to use as they turn in announcements to the church office. This form can be very helpful for getting the facts about events. It can serve as a checklist to make sure all of the essential information is in place.

Have a place for testimonies and always include a gospel presentation

Every bulletin should have a short piece about how someone can come to trust Jesus as his or her Savior. Upbeat, short stories that talk about the love of Jesus at work in people's lives do a better job of effectively marketing the message of Christianity than do pictures of churches or pieces of clip art that now decorate many bulletin covers.

Presenting the gospel is what we are all about, and the bulletin ought to have a place for it. You can use a short verse of scripture (John 3:16 pretty much says it all), or include a longer narrative that varies with the time of year. For example, one church uses the narrative below at Christmas:

> In the midst of the gifts and goodies we are all enjoying at this time of year, remember the message of Christmas is that God came to Earth in the form of a person—Jesus of Nazareth. Jesus grew up not only to become the greatest teacher and miracle worker the world had ever seen, but also to die a unique death.

> In His death, Jesus was not a victim of evil men. Jesus willingly gave up His life and died on the cross so that He could pay the penalty for our sins. His death was His choice and His story doesn't end with His death. Jesus rose from the dead after three days and by doing so, demonstrated that He was God.

> When we believe that Jesus died for our sins, accept the forgiveness He offers us, and decide to follow Him, Jesus promises to forgive us and gives us eternal life.

> If you'd like to have your sins forgiven; if you'd like to be at peace with your God; if you'd like to live forever, tell Jesus you are a sinner and you need His salvation. Ask Him to come into your life to be your Savior and Lord.

> After you do that, please read the Bible to learn how to live as a Christian. Talk to God daily in prayer. Go to a church and get to know other followers of Jesus and grow in your faith.

You can also modify your bulletin's gospel presentation to fit the season of the year. For example, at Christmas you can talk about receiving a free gift, at Easter you can challenge people to a new life, during Father's Day you can talk about how your heavenly Father wants you to become part of God's forever family.

The results of a gospel presentation in a church bulletin

One woman decided to include in her bulletin a brief gospel presentation similar to the one above. She shared with me that one of the men in her church had to go to prison for a time. In order to keep him in touch with the church, she regularly sent him the bulletin.

The man wrote to her and said, "Thank you so much for sending me the church bulletin. It has helped me feel like I'm not forgotten here. I also want you to know that I've led several inmates here in prison to the Lord. I used the church bulletin as my gospel tract."

Taking the time to squeeze the gospel presentation between all the announcements and news isn't easy. It was probably just as hard for the church secretary to do it as it will be for you as you put your bulletin together week after week. But what great results! The eternal destinies of men were changed by this church secretary's office publications. It is worth the effort.

Work hard on your church bulletins. They are difficult, repetitive, and sometimes boring to do, but heaven will be a different place depending on the work you do on them each week.

Bulletin inserts

"What about church bulletin inserts?" I'm often asked this question as I teach my ministry communication and marketing seminars. The person who asks it usually isn't prepared for my response. I know I am expected to say, "Church bulletins should never have inserts. They are messy, too much work, and half of them end up on the floor anyway." Most church office workers would love it if I told them to never do a bulletin insert again. But I can't tell them that.

> *Positioning means determining exactly what niche your offering is intended to fill.*[43]
> —Jay Conrad Levinson, *Guerilla Marketing*

The reason is that church bulletin inserts are one of the best marketing pieces your church has for the ongoing ministries in your church. If their real value is understood and they are created and used properly, then bulletin inserts are huge assets.

Bulletin inserts are perfect vehicles for niche marketing. Niche marketing targets well-defined interest groups with sales presentations designed to speak specifically to that group. For example, new parents are a clearly defined niche market. When a couple first has a baby, they need all sorts of things. Direct mail marketers of diapers, strollers, infant toys, and all sorts of other baby articles don't send out large mailings to every possible person. Instead, marketers buy mailing lists of new parents and market specifically to them. Niche marketing, when it functions well, greatly benefits both the buyer and seller. It targets real needs, it doesn't waste anybody's time, and the exchange of goods and services goes smoothly.

Think in terms of niche marketing in your church

For most churches, not every program or event in the church appeals to everyone. Moms of preschoolers don't need to know all the details of what the college group is doing for the summer. However, church bulletins often list events for all groups and it's difficult to find what applies to a specific group. In addition, many bulletins aren't large enough to contain all the information people need.

Sometimes the phrase, "call the church office for more information" is used as a way to encourage people to find the information that they need, but few people will call. The result is that many worthwhile ministries are under-attended.

Bulletin inserts can solve this problem. Think of a bulletin insert as a mini brochure or billboard that advertises a specific ministry to a narrowly defined targeted market. People will read only the particular insert that is of importance to them. This is the information that people will keep. They will probably pull the insert that interests them out of the bulletin and take it home to post on the refrigerator. Once the message makes it to the refrigerator, people will most likely act on it.

Tips for making bulletin inserts effective

- Be consistent in the use of both ink and paper colors for inserts. For example, always use pink for nursery news, green for missions, electric orange for high school, etc. Consistency allows people to find the information they need quickly.

- Again, think mini-billboard. Don't waste time writing lots of wordy explanations. Cut to the core of the message and just print that.

- When designing inserts, make those Five Ws large and easy to see. Remember, the Five Ws are who, what, where, when, and why. Include the start time, end time, location, directions, contact phone number, cost, etc. Be sure to include *all* of the details.

- Tell people exactly what you want them to do, such as call to sign up, donate something, or attend a meeting.

- Use one large piece of clip art appropriate to the subject, rather than an assortment of little ones. Select clip art that emphasizes the message of your insert rather than just being decorative.

- Use easy-to-read typefaces for key information. It's OK to use a wild and crazy typeface for the headlines or for catchy slogans, but if something is hard to read, many people just won't bother.

- Print on only one side of the paper. Most inserts will end up on the refrigerator where they can only be viewed from one side.

A new name might help

Don't call them bulletin inserts anymore. Call them *Refrigerator Reminders*. Many churches made this name change and actually have that title on the top of the page. Some churches provide refrigerator reminders for specific events, and some provide a page that summarizes all the events going on in the church that week.

Some churches really have fun with this idea and create a special refrigerator magnet that communicates all the basic church contact information, and includes the church slogan or mission statement.

CHAPTER 12:

Niche Newsletters

A positive trend in some churches is the development of niche newsletters. The idea is that the church no longer puts all of its effort into creating one overall newsletter for the entire church. That may still happen, but your church may have a more effective marketing ministry if you decide to create niche newsletters for outreach.

> *Strong newsletters specialize. If you have more than one audience, consider more than one newsletter . . . As an alternative, produce special inserts for specific portions of the audience.*[44]
> —Mark Beach,
> *Editing Your Newsletter*

How niche newsletters work

- Begin by identifying a group that the church wants to reach more aggressively than it has in the past. Examples include parents of teenagers, parents of grade school children, singles, or working couples.

- Recruit a publication team made up of volunteers to help in this venture. Have the team create a newsletter specifically for the target group, remembering to speak primarily to the needs, questions, and concerns of the target group.

- The niche newsletter will present how the church can help meet the target group's needs. Make enough copies not only for people currently attending the church but also for current members to give them out to unchurched friends.

- Do not emphasize the greatness of the church in this publication. Focus instead on meeting needs.

Examples of niche newsletters
The Parent Gazette

The church that produced *The Parent Gazette* realized that if it tried to create one newsletter for both parents and teenagers, the newsletter wouldn't be especially effective for either group. In this case, the teenagers decided to do their own newsletter, while the staff worked on a newsletter for parents. *The Parent Gazette* not only updated parents concerning youth group activities, it also contained articles that gave parenting advice. Some of the article titles included: "Why Teenagers Leave," "When Junior Highers Have Crushes," and "The Stress Factor." Many parents today don't know how to parent, and they are scared. If your church can position itself as a resource to help parents raise their kids, then that creates powerful appeal to parents for your church as a whole.

The Home Page

This newsletter was created for the parents of elementary-age children. Again, it contained the expected updates and information about what was going on at the church. It also included lots of helpful tips for raising kids today, including tips on discipline, how to teach kids values and manners, and fun ideas that take little time and money. Again, the church worked hard to let parents know that the church wanted to partner with them and help them be better parents.

The Couples Connection

The Couples Connection is a newsletter for working professional couples. I found it at a very large church where I was doing a seminar and I snatched it up. It had articles entitled, "Making Time for Romance," "Communicating on the Run," and "Affair-Proof your Christian Marriage." Great stuff.

Single Strategies

Despite the name, this niche newsletter isn't about dating. It provides all sorts of life strategies, including tax tips, adventure vacations for singles, suggestions for single parents, and the activities of the singles group at the church. This newsletter is upbeat and positive.

Overall tips for niche newsletters

- Be sure that the information provided is genuinely useful to the niche group you target, whether the group attends church or not.

- Don't be shy about inviting people to activities at your church. For example, one of the most natural ways to do this is through an article on budgeting for your target group. After the article runs, advertise a workshop on the topic offered by the church.

- How the niche newsletter looks and its production quality isn't nearly as important as its content. Produce newsletters quickly and easily using a template from Microsoft Publisher.® There are many upbeat, easy to use template designs in that program. While design is important, looks are not nearly as important as content issues, such as screening out church jargon and judgmental, negative attitudes. Remember, the gospel message is a message of good news. Church niche newsletters need to reflect good news in every way.

- Create niche newsletters not only as a part of your church's Ministry Marketing efforts directed at groups within the church, but also as intentional Ministry Marketing outreach. Print lots of copies and remind members to give newsletters to friends as a gentle way to introduce them to your church.

SECTION FOUR:

Strategic Implementation of Easy Ministry Marketing

We've looked at the foundation for Ministry Marketing, the characteristics of good Ministry Marketing, and finally we've looked closely at some essential Ministry Marketing publications.

One more area of advice is needed— practical tips for implementing these Ministry Marketing ideas in your church, and that is what this section is about.

In it you will see that easy Ministry Marketing is:

And of the children of Issachar, which were men that had understanding of the times, to know what Israel ought to do; the heads of them were two hundred; and all their brethren were at their commandment. (KJV)

All these men understood the temper of the times and knew the best course for Israel to take . . .(NLT)

. . . men who understood both the times and Israel's duties . . . (MSG)
—Various translations of
1 Chronicles 12:32

Persistent You have to repeat the message so many more times than seems sensible or possible for a response or for it to really make a difference in the behavior of your target audience.

Planned The biggest mistake Ministry Marketers make in planning is they forget to plan what to do once people actually get to an event. A plan for follow-up is essential. It ensures that your hard work will be successful over the long term.

Programmed You can't create all the great Ministry Marketing materials you need all by yourself. This chapter will introduce you to some great resources that can help.

Publicity Proactive The media won't come to you, but it needs you for stories. Learn how to build a positive, continuing relationship with the media and, if all else fails, how to create your own media.

Pervasive The best Ministry Marketing materials in the world will fail if the person staffing the Welcome Center is grumpy. Use the information here to learn how to make the Welcome Center work.

Partnering You need a team. You can't do it alone. I will tell you what you need to do to keep your Ministry Marketing staff and volunteers working with you.

Properly Equipped I'm not going to bore you with an overwhelming number of options. Instead, I'll share two tools that I consider essential to Ministry Marketing success.

Prayer Saturated This isn't really about giving advice. But it is about three stories of how prayer can accomplish our goal of reaching people with the message of the good news.

We will tackle two of each of these characteristics in each of the chapters that follow.

CHAPTER 13:

Easy Ministry Marketing Is Persistent and Planned

The importance of persistence

Remember, as we discussed extensively early in this book, the medium isn't the message—the message is the message. People must hear the message again and again for it to stick in their minds. Current marketing theory says that people need to hear or see a message a minimum of seven times before they take action. Your church or ministry needs to get its marketing message out to individuals many more times than that if you expect to see results.

> *The winners are those that employ . . . an integrated marketing solution, and drive value through a range in interrelated and supporting initiatives encompassing a number of media channels including direct mail, print and TV ads, interactive and e-mail marketing, tele-services, promotions and others.*
> —John F. Fastrem,
> from an editorial in *Ad Age*

Persistence is key to success in Ministry Marketing

Many Ministry Marketing messages fail because the church or ministry doing the marketing doesn't repeat its message enough. For the church, a failed marketing message means that fewer people attend events, and thus miss that first step toward spiritual growth. The following story illustrates what happens at many churches.

A church office worker approached me at a seminar break and said, "Our church choir director is so discouraged. The choir worked really hard to put on a great spring concert and almost nobody came. She told me, 'I'm never doing this again. People just don't care!' What should I tell her?"

"I understand the pain of people not coming," I replied. "But tell me, how did you advertise the concert?"

"Well," she replied, "we put it in the bulletin *two* times!"

Apparently the powers that be at this church required a special dispensation to put anything in the bulletin more than once.

"Oh, my goodness," I said, "people didn't show up, not because they didn't care. Most of them didn't know it was going on!"

False assumptions concerning repetition

Somehow we assume that just because what we are doing in the church is *really important,* people will attend. This is a false assumption, not because of any lack of spirituality in the church, but it's just the nature of people today that something has to be repeated many times for it to somehow penetrate the fog of information overload we all face daily, no matter how important it is.

We assume everybody sees the message every time we put it out there. We forget that not everybody is there every Sunday—remember, only twenty percent of your folks are there every Sunday. We forget *nobody* sees the PR and listing to events as much as we do. We forget not everyone has e-mail or checks the web site frequently for updates.

We limit our repetitions because we allow the one or two people who are there every Sunday, and who are the self-appointed critics and complainers of everything that is printed or announced in the church, to set the agenda for our communication strategy. You know who I am talking about. Every church has these dear folks. Moses was able to send snakes to destroy the grumblers in the camp (Numbers 21). We don't have that option, but don't let them set the marketing strategy for the church.

Tips on persistent marketing

Be consistent, not original

One of the comments I hear frequently is, "If I state my announcement in the same way week after week, or if I write it in the same way in the bulletin and in the newsletter, my readers will get bored and won't read it."

This is a totally incorrect assumption. Readers do not get bored. Readers are far more likely to get confused. Even if they see an announcement as many times as you do (almost none of them will), changes in presentation lead people to think you are talking about a different event.

Pay attention to secular advertising campaigns. Successful companies come up with a slogan or marketing campaign and repeat the same thing again and again and again. Don't change the message; change the method you use to communicate the message.

Take advantage of a multi-channel approach

We have a marvelous palette of tools to use to present Ministry Marketing messages. Use them all. I cannot repeat enough that there is no one perfect or most successful marketing tool. Use web sites and PowerPoint®, and also use postcards, newsletters, and personal phone calls. Get your message out through as many channels as you can, as many times as you can, and hope somebody is paying attention when they get it.

Think ad campaign

The following story illustrates how a multi-channel approach can work in marketing a ministry event.

My pastor husband had worked for two years to get a national seminar about small groups scheduled at our church. When he finally got a date confirmed that would work for both our church and the seminar presenters, we only had one month to market the event.

I called the woman who published the church calendar (the senior pastor and staff had already approved the seminar) and she informed me, "I'll put it on the calendar, but nobody is going to come to your event."

"Why do you say that?" I asked. She replied by telling me of a number of other events that were scheduled at the church for the same day. However, it was a church of about 1,800 people and there were plenty of people to go around. The church office worker concluded by telling me that one of the events scheduled for the same day as our seminar was a free workshop led by a nationally famous author. It had just been confirmed and the event was going to be free because a video shoot of the workshop was scheduled that day as well. Our event was somewhat costly.

"So, nobody will come to your event," she repeated.

I took this as a challenge.

I'd recently been studying advertising campaigns and multi-channel communication and I thought, "If I can't make this work for my church, how can I teach other churches what to do?" Making this event work out, then, became a trial for me on several levels.

Before I describe what I did, let me assure you that what I did anybody can do. The marketing materials that I used were very simple. I created the publication using Microsoft Publisher®'s ready-made templates. The materials were printed very inexpensively on a RISO, using neon green paper with black ink. Churches that can afford it could have produced fancier, full-color marketing pieces, but that was not essential to getting the job done.

The marketing procedure:

1. I obtained from the church a list of ninety people who had shown interested in small-group leadership training. I printed sets of mailing labels for this group.

2. I created a very simple brochure using the MS Publisher® brochure template. From this "advertising campaign" experience I have learned to create a brochure first because the brochure organizes the Five Ws for me (the who, what, when, where, and why). With this essential information in place, all I had to do was simply cut and paste it into other publication pieces and on to the web.

3. The first piece I sent out was a letter from my husband to each of the people on the list, inviting them to the seminar. I enclosed the brochure with the letter. The brochure was also placed on an information table in the courtyard of the church.

4. Cutting and pasting information and using similar designs, I created two bulletin inserts to be used over the next two

weeks. The third week we were going to insert the brochure in the bulletin.

5. I also created four bulletin announcements. The reason for both inserts and announcements is because announcements in the bulletin are read during the church service. Hopefully, inserts are taken home and placed on the refrigerator. Even though people get the bulletin and the bulletin inserts at the same time, they are two totally separate publications with totally different purposes.

6. I created three sets of postcards, one to be sent out each week until the seminar, starting the week after people received the letter. Only the ninety people on the mailing list got this postcard.

I created all of these pieces at the same time, got them ready to go, and delivered them to the church workroom with directions for distribution attached. I did the project this way because of my travel schedule, but I've tried to do others the same way even when I wasn't traveling. By doing everything all at once (cut, paste, and create the various publications at one time using the same color paper and ink for printing), the work is easier and faster. Everything was ready and I took off traveling, praying as I went. This was a very important event for my husband's ministry and for the life of the church.

The response to the campaign

The week before the event, I checked my voicemail messages and there was a panicked message from the woman taking the registration for the small-group seminar. She informed me that the national ministry people did not believe the registration numbers that she had given them were correct.

I called the national ministry people to assure them that our numbers were correct, and I asked as politely as I was able, "Why didn't you believe us?"

"Because nobody in your state has ever gotten such high numbers to attend our events," was the answer.

What great news! The event was extremely successful, attendance was overflowing, folks loved it, and many small groups started as a result.

Additional lessons and tips for church ad campaigns

- Because all the marketing for the event was done on the neon green paper, and because there were a number of events going on at the church that day, what color do you suppose we used for directional signs, informing people how to get from the parking lot to our event? Neon green, of course!

- Several people came up to me the day of the event and said something like, "You know, it wasn't until I got that third postcard that it finally clicked—you guys were doing this training today." Even though I would have liked to scream, "Why couldn't you respond to the first mailing?" there is just no reason to get upset. People don't respond to just one postcard. That's life today.

- Just because something is from the church and it's important to us for them to attend, that doesn't make the letter jump out of the pile of junk mail everybody gets every day. It took a saturation of marketing pieces from a variety of channels to move people to respond.

What doesn't work in event marketing

Remember the big deal national speaker videotaping event going on at the church on the same day? While I worked hard doing all sorts of little things to promote our costly, time-intensive training event, the leaders in charge of marketing the video shoot assumed that because the speaker was so well known, and because the event was free, they didn't need to do much to advertise it.

All the advertising for the competing event consisted of a fancy and complete announcement in the bulletin that ran for two weeks before the event. It was a nice announcement, but that was it. Out of a congregation of around 1,800 people, approximately twenty people showed up.

Ministry Marketing lessons to consider from the low turnout

- Few people remember the details of an event if the last time they saw it was on the previous Sunday in the bulletin.

- Attendance would have been higher for the video shoot if a postcard reminder had arrived on Thursday, reminding people of the seminar on Saturday. E-mails would have helped also.

- The video shoot planners should not have assumed that just because the speaker was well known, just because it was free, and just because it was really good for the people, people would flock to the event. It doesn't matter how great an event is, or how attractive the cost is, or how it will benefit people. These things will not determine the attendance at the event. What determines the turnout is how *you* market the event. All other things equal (or not), that's what will get people there.

Easy Ministry Marketing Is Planned Progressively

Much of Ministry Marketing is designed to get people *to* an event. While increasing attendance is important, it isn't all that marketing, when approached as a ministry, entails.

Lots of work results in little long-term results

A story was shared with me about a new church that wanted to reach out to the

> *Three principles of utmost importance to the success of [marketing] planning in congregations*
>
> *(1) Keep it simple . . .*
> *(2) Keep it natural . . .*
> *(3) People tend to support what they have helped to create.*[45]
>
> —From *Marketing for Congregations*

131

community at Easter. The church was already doing quite well. It met regularly at an elementary school and had grown to more than 200 in attendance. But the members really wanted to give a big push and reach out to more people.

The excitement over initial results

The church worked hard to increase community involvement and it succeeded. Merchants put up posters and the media gave the church lots of exposure. Easter came and the church of 200 had more than 1,500 at the Easter service, which had to be held at the local high school gym. It was a fantastic service.

The letdown

The week after Easter, the usual 200 people were the only people at church. It was a huge disappointment. The woman who shared this story was between laughing and crying as she said, "Now I understand what happened! We didn't give any of the visitors follow-up material! We didn't tell them the high school was *not* where we met regularly. We didn't even think about it. We worked so hard just making it happen and cleaning up after it did. If we'd driven over to the high school parking lot on the Sunday after Easter, we probably would have found hundreds of cars and people wandering around wondering where the church went."

She also said they hadn't gotten people to fill out a visitor response card because they ran out of time as they prepared for the event.

Plan for post-event follow up first

I've heard similar stories repeated constantly. It's another occupational hazard for those of us working in the church: We assume that people will come to a bridge event, an outreach event, or a special event, and if they like us they will automatically come to our regular church events. This doesn't happen. This doesn't happen because if you are doing outreach events to unchurched people they have *no* idea what your church does on a regular basis. They don't know what churches do. They might assume your church is a nice organization that gives neat parties for the community around the holidays.

They won't know what else goes on unless you tell them. You need to let them know immediately after the event, in specific detail, what else your church does. They need to leave with an invitation that invites them to what you do on a regular basis and invites them to take the next step of connection with your church. In addition, you need to have captured their names and contact information so you can stay in contact with them on a continuing basis and build on the relationship you have begun.

You also need to decide how to do this *before* you plan anything else for your special event. If you don't, you will most likely get so busy in the PR for the event and in the details of putting it on that these Ministry Marketing activities will be forgotten—that is the simple reality of working in the church. But these Ministry Marketing publications are not optional, last-minute pieces. They are the key to the success of your outreach event.

Below is an example of how you might market a Fall Harvest Festival with suggestions for Ministry Marketing activities you can do before, during, and after the event. This is Ministry Marketing that is planned strategically for more than simply getting people to an event. You want to use any outreach event as the start of a relationship with your church.

Remember, just because you hold a great neighborhood event and people enjoy it, don't assume that means they will show up with their kids for Sunday School next week. Most of them don't even know an event such as "Sunday School" happens. You've got to plan Ministry Marketing for every step of your interactions for people to respond in a way that will ultimately change their lives. None of these recommended activities are difficult to do, but you need to plan ahead to make certain they get done.

Fall Harvest Festival Follow-up Marketing Suggestions

You've done all the right advertising: you sent out postcards, you've taken door-hangers[46] around your community to invite people, you're in the community calendar and on the radio, you've got volunteers, and a great event is about to happen.

But don't stop now! Don't miss some of your best Ministry Marketing opportunities that should take place during and after the event. It is critical to do these things because you don't just want people to come to your church for a fun evening. You want to use this event as the beginning of a relationship with your visitors. You want to get them coming back to your church and you want to influence their lives for eternity. To do that takes more than one fun night.

Capture connection information

Do all you can to capture the names, street, and e-mail addresses of the people who attend your events. One way to do this is to have a card that folks may fill out for fun prizes at drawings you'll hold during the evening. Have lots of people at welcome tables helping visitors fill these out, so visitors don't have to wait in long lines to get in on the fun. No marketer who intends to keep his or her job would ever host an event without capturing the names of the people who attended.

Exit and after-the-event communications

When people leave your event, be sure you have some sort of goodie bag for them to take home. If the event is a Harvest Festival, you might include some yummy candy and a Halloween gospel tract. The American Tract Society (www.ATStracts.org) has some great resources for all holiday occasions.

In addition, be sure you have enclosed something that talks about what your church does on a regular basis and what you want your visitors to do next. Print this on appropriately colored paper, and write it in a cheery, upbeat style. The note might say something like this:

We're so glad you came to our Harvest Festival and we trust you enjoyed yourself!

We really care about kids at [YOUR CHURCH NAME] and your experience was just a sample of the fun and exciting ways we show that caring spirit.

For more positive times for your children, please join us next Sunday at our Kids Kove for fun and lessons with a purpose.

We meet at [time, location, etc]. Please know we carefully screen our children's workers and provide conscientious and caring supervision for all children's events. For more information, please visit our web site: www.yourchurchkidsection or call Miss Susie, our children's director at 555-555-5555.

Repeat this message in postcards and through follow-up e-mails using the information you collected at sign-in time. You aren't being too pushy in doing this—you are helping introduce people to a relationship with Jesus. You are connecting people to your church, where further steps on their spiritual pilgrimage can take place on a weekly basis, and not only at holiday special events.

General tips on strategically planning your Ministry Marketing materials

Now that you know what to do with the people once you get them to events, step back and evaluate your plan for publicity, paying particular attention to your schedule. For any event that involves a significant amount of time or money (a major conference, camps for kids, etc.) begin advertising the date and the cost six months beforehand. Advertise in the church calendar, bulletin, newsletter, and on the church's web site. A simple "Upcoming Events" section works well for this.

One month ahead of the event, begin intensive advertising as described in the section above about how to do an ad campaign. This is the time to send out postcards and e-mails, use bulletin inserts and announcements, and provide more details on the web and in church multimedia presentations. Needless to say, not every event gets the same amount of publicity. For some events, the church office can handle the marketing effort on behalf of the entire church. In other situations, individual departments can take over the responsibility.

For every event that you want people to attend, send a postcard and an e-mail a few days before the event. If possible, also make a phone call, either a personal one or by using PhoneTree.[47] The number of responses will increase significantly if you do these three things.

135

Once again, have your plan to capture names and how you will follow up after the event in place before you do anything else.

Be prepared for both positive and negative responses

Know that if you do all of these things you will experience an increase in both positive responses and negative responses.

On the positive side, you will have far greater attendance for the initial event and following it. People will connect with your church and come to know Jesus. But all the responses won't be positive. You will also hear the complainers complain:

"You put that in the bulletin *four* times."

"You are killing trees to do up all these bulletin inserts. And they make a mess."

"I'm tired of seeing that same PowerPoint® slide about the youth retreat. Isn't once enough for them to get the message? The music was loud enough no one can forget it."

Just smile and pray. This is a test to help you grow in Christian love and patience. You can try to talk to folks about the importance of repetition in marketing, but they may or may not care. As stated earlier, you cannot allow negative folks to set your Ministry Marketing agenda.

CHAPTER 14:

Easy Ministry Marketing Is Programmed and Publicity Proactive

In order to manage all of your church's Ministry Marketing projects, you may not be able to create every item yourself. The first part of this chapter is about how to use professional, paid, design help and resources, and programmed Ministry Marketing, when appropriate.

> *Focus on the parts of your community that God is calling you to reach and send mail fliers, postcards and/or invitations to homes in driving range of your church.*
> —Advice from
> www.outreach.com

I am sensitive to the budget constraints of small churches, inner city churches, and any church struggling to meet its budget today. The information in this section is not meant to suggest that everyone has to make use of professional resources or that it is appropriate for every church. You can create everything you need using the tools I have already described such as MS Publisher® and a RISO. There is, however, a world to win for Jesus and it's important to check out every resource available, even if it's just to gather ideas.

Available programs are costly, so secure funding first

Churches are like families in that both churches and families spend money on what is important to them. The priorities of every family are accurately recorded in its checkbook, and sometimes church leadership needs to challenge families to take a look at what those priorities reveal.

There are people in every congregation who can easily help fund professional marketing expenses, if they are convinced of the need. Money is never really a problem in equipping God's people for outreach; wrong priorities in people are the problem. As a church leader, you may need to pray for wisdom and grace, and schedule some face-to-face time with key individuals in your church in order to challenge them to practice their spiritual gift of giving. People may need to hear that for the price of one less car for the family or the cost of a designer piece of clothing, a new pair of shoes or a new purse, or money saved by taking a vacation at home instead of going on a cruise, your church could purchase some pretty significant marketing tools.

I'm addressing this issue of funding up front because many of the resources I'm going to list (not all, but many) are not cheap. Also, to be effective, repetition is what will make them work best, and that adds significantly to the cost. You will *not* have success with these programs if you just use them one time. Fancy printing, a catchy slogan, or full color does not negate the need for repetition.

Assume you've got the money, now look at the options

This is where it gets fun. Go online and look at all the great resources that are available. In the next section there is an extensive list of resources. Request samples. Let your imagination go crazy.

You may not use professional products for every Ministry Marketing program, but in some cases, professional services may be just the thing to kick start an outreach program. It may save you time and money by using materials created by a professional design firm, as opposed to hiring additional staff. Professional services may provide you with a polished look that is appropriate for your target audience.

As you consider these programs, don't feel you have to use them exclusively. You may decide to use parts of one, get some ideas from another, and do some projects yourself. Even if you decide not to use any of these projects and services, you'll learn new techniques and get great ideas that will inspire your own projects as you look at how professionals do marketing.

Some of the vendors below have seminars that help you make better use of their products. I encourage you to attend these seminars and learn what you can. Of course, they will want to sell you the products they produce when you go to their seminars. Selling good things to enrich ministry isn't a bad thing; everybody has to pay the rent. If cost is an issue now that prevents you from attending, it may not be in the future. Remember what you learn for future situations when these services may be just what your church needs.

Some choices in programmed marketing for print

These sources are primarily programmed materials for printed pieces. There are many additional resources for Ministry Marketing. Tools are available in multi-media formats and for TV and radio advertising. To find these, your denominational web sites list some of the best resources. Some include:

United Methodist Communications: http://www.umcom.org (United Methodist).

Church Advertising Resources: http://www.namb.net/ads (North American Mission Board).

Lutheran, ECLA: http://www.ecla.org.

Technologies for Worship: http://www.tfwm.com (numerous multi-media resources).

Details Direct and Outreach Marketing

Details Direct and Outreach Marketing are the companies with which I am most familiar. They are based on opposite ends of the country and that is reflected in their designs. Details is in the South, and Outreach is a California company. Both are great, but one may appeal to your audience more than the other. They both have quality products and I recommend them highly.

www.detailsdirect.org

Details Direct is part of a family of companies that includes *E-zekiel Web Sites*, one of the best web site sources for churches. It is also one of the major companies that produces worship guides, direct mail pieces, logo creation, and identity building programs. I've had lots of positive feedback about this group, and many positive comments from people in my seminars who have used their materials.

Note of caution: be really careful when you type in the URL for this web site. It is so easy and automatic to hit .com instead of .org. If you do that, (and I'm cautioning you because I do it about every other time I go to the web site) you will get the web site for Details magazine, a men's lifestyle magazine—it's not a bad one, but it also doesn't sell anything related to church marketing.

www.outreach.com

Outreach Marketing is the big kahuna of outreach marketing materials. They have a huge catalog filled with shells for bulletins, outreach cards, invitation cards, door hangers, banners, brochure shells, and ways to distribute and display these items. They are the official creators of materials for many Purpose-Driven programs and for the outreach materials for *The Passion of the Christ*. They publish a great magazine on outreach, sponsor a national conference on outreach in November, plus they sponsor several outreach and evangelism seminars each year.

Additional programmed print resources worth checking out

These additional print resources offer similar products, though the selections are not as extensive. They look promising, but I haven't been personally involved with their material. Check out the things that you believe will work best for you and your church.

Faith Span:
> http://www.faithspan.com

Church Marketing Solutions:
> http://www.churchmarketing.org

Breakthrough Church:
> http://www.breakthroughchurch.com

Mustard Seed Studio:
> http://www.mustardseedstudio.com

Compass Outreach Media:
> http://www.compassoutreachmedia.com

Warner Press:
> http://www.warnerpress.org

Easy Ministry Marketing Is Publicity Proactive

Christians often complain about how they are treated by the media. They complain they don't get the coverage they want; they complain about how Christians are presented; they lament that so many unchristian agendas are given primetime coverage.

Though this frustration is understandable, bad or inadequate coverage of the Christian church is not inevitable. With computers, desktop publishing, and the Internet, we no longer have an excuse to complain. You can generate media coverage for your church or ministry, and you can create your own media.

Take advantage of the available media sources

In order to make the media work for you, you must understand how it works. I was religion reporter for the *Colorado Springs Sun* newspaper for a number of years, and it never ceased to amaze me the ways that churches approached the media.

> *Journalists don't want to help you communicate with your target market. They couldn't care less about your target market. But journalists are happy to use any good story that you're willing to write for them, and if your product gets mentioned or your marketing manager gets quoted as a result, that's not a problem. So the secret, the key, the essence, of good publicity is to develop stories with effective hooks and give them away to overworked journalists who are eager for a little help from volunteers like you.*[48]
>
> —Alexander Hiam,
> *Marketing for Dummies*

Almost weekly, I received at least one article delivered with the threat that God would judge me if I didn't use the article exactly as it was written. I'm a believer in Jesus and I wanted to report true and good news, but such tactics did not work with me. Similar demands have far more negative consequences with secular reporters.

Newspaper reporters, especially those who cover special interest areas such as religion, are not out looking for stories or news about religion. The topic of religion is not a priority for most media outlets. Reporters rarely have time to research stories, so they often write stories based on press releases that they receive. This means that you can't expect reporters to come to you looking for stories about your exciting church events. You've got to get the information to reporters, and you've got to do it regularly, in exactly the way they want it, and you must do it with a smile and a lot of prayer.

You *have to give them news items*

There are two primary areas that your church should be continually giving to your local religion reporters. These are:

> 1. Notices for free calendar space
> 2. Press releases.

The following are additional tips for making the most of each of them. Though they may not seem significant, having your church even briefly mentioned in community calendars or news updates each week will create "product awareness" of your church in your community.

God can greatly use these seemingly small acts of marketing faithfulness. For example, an unchurched woman might barely notice as she regularly skims the community calendar that your church offers a Grief Recovery Workshop every six weeks. But her father dies suddenly of a heart attack and she doesn't know what to do— then she remembers your church helps people who are grieving. There is a much greater chance she will call your church at that time than if you never let the community know you hold the classes.

Calendar space notices

Many newspapers publish free calendar notices of churches' activities. Television and radio stations also often provide free public service announcements or community calendars as well. Call your local newspapers, television, and radio stations to find out how to have your events included. Fill out the forms exactly as instructed and be sure to turn them in by the required deadlines. Be creative with how you name your event or service. Include whether or not childcare will be provided. Edit church-specific language if you intend the message to reach the unchurched.

Press release tips

Prior to sending in press releases, try to talk to the religion reporter to find out what sort of news or stories are of interest to him or her. When you call, always ask if this is a good time to answer a few questions. If a reporter is on deadline, be respectful and ask when would be the best time to call back. Always be very considerate of a reporter's time. With the exception of really large media outlets, most reporters are greatly underpaid and work demanding, pressured schedules. If you are kind to them, they will remember it. If you are rude or demanding because your news is from your church and you consider your schedule more important than their schedule, they will remember that also.

As to format, in the past, many books on marketing have given precise examples of how press releases should be submitted. There is no standard format today, other than the general advice to be brief and include complete information.

Different media in different areas want press releases submitted in different ways. Some want e-mails, some faxes, some still like printed pages. Ask about format preferences and avenues for submission and then do *exactly* as instructed.

Find out what type of ministry event would merit additional coverage. Be kind, courteous, and don't ever tell someone, "God says you have to publish this story, or else." Even then, you'll have many humbling experiences when you deal with the press. Everyone thinks his or her story is most important, but reporters seldom agree.

However, reporters have to fill a set number of column inches or minutes on the air each week. They need your press releases and your stories. They can't make up church news or events, and they rely on interested parties to tell them about what is going on. You never know what they will use, but if you don't send them information, you'll never get any coverage.

In a number of my seminars, various church administrators have told me that with the permission of the local religion reporter they fax, mail, or e-mail the church newsletter to the reporter regularly. From that the reporter pulls whatever news and calendar dates that seem interesting and sometimes calls to follow up and do additional stories on upcoming events.

If you want to be really brave

There is one additional way you can get coverage from the media: Be willing to become a spokesperson for Christianity.

Reporters like to get opinions that reflect the various positions people hold when controversial issues come up. For example, if there is a city ordinance vote concerning an adult bookstore, a reporter will want a quote from a local pastor on why churches are protesting. Volunteering to be a spokesperson for the church is a very serious commitment. You must know God wants you to do it, have a tough skin, and have a gracious spirit. You will be misquoted. You will get nasty letters and phone calls—especially if you speak the Word of God clearly and truly. Sadly, much of the criticism may come from fellow believers. But being a Christian spokesperson is an incredible opportunity to get the Christian viewpoint into the public arena.

Be realistic in your expectations

In this and every area of interaction with the media, *never* retaliate if you feel you have been misquoted or that a story is unfair. Countercultural groups know that any news coverage is good coverage. It gets your cause in the public eye and you are seen as a participating force in the world.

The church in America has become touchy about its image, and this is a problem. Few reporters seek out Christian spokespersons for comments on world issues. Touchy pastors with big egos have been known to burn reporters, and reporters don't want to bother with them. People with messages other than the Christian gospel are quite happy to fill the gap.

Be willing to be made a fool for Christ. Remember, the Apostle Paul was stoned and kicked out of almost every new area where he preached. But in every town that he left because of "unfair media coverage," he spoke the gospel message clearly and he left behind believers.

Be aware that ninety-nine percent of the press releases or editorials that you send to media outlets will not make the final cut. However, reporters do read press releases. Over time, they get to know you and will contact you or write something if they are interested. Editorials are also read. After six months and no response, a reporter may contact you because of something you submitted. Readers may initially label you as a "nut case," but your argument sticks with them. Your work is never wasted. The media is not fair or balanced, no matter what certain networks claim. Every media outlet has an agenda; some are just more obvious than others. Many small town reporters can be lazy and petty. You've got to be nice to them and consistently supply them with news in the format they want. Eventually, some of it will be published.

Create your own media

Dealing with the media may seem like too much trouble, but the good news is you don't have to wait for local newspapers, TV, and radio stations to tell your story. Every single church with a computer has a printing press at its disposal. You can use this powerful communication tool to influence your community. If you have a web site, you can theoretically reach the world.

When you put together the church publication budget, don't just plan publicity for your church community. Most of the folks who go to your church believe the same things you do. On significant community issues, why not send out information to the community at large? Be aware of the rules for nonprofit agencies, but also know that folks in your church are free to act on their own.

Ministry Marketing by individuals

- Encourage church members to send postcards. Postcards are a great way to present a few important points of an issue, remind people to vote, encourage people to think about an issue, or let people know that the church is there to help with their problems. You can print a door hanger telling people that God loves them and inviting folks to get introduced to their Creator by coming to your church.

- Create a *Good News Newsletter* for the larger community instead of only publishing newsletters for your church community. Tell the good news of what's happening at your church and how it can benefit everyone. Tell your church neighbors how the Bible gives advice on parenting, money management, and communication. Let people know about Mom's Morning Out, aerobics classes, and the community softball team that your church sponsors. If you are concerned about values in your community, start a publication that celebrates the values you want to see grow.

- Printed pieces can direct people to your church's web site, where they can find detailed discussions of issues and become more interested in your church. In order to use the web for outreach, consider a site separate from your church's main web site. Design this additional site with seekers in mind, and provide links to your church's main web site.

- Create electronic versions of the gospel story, or create an outreach newsletter to email to people. Be sure to include a working op-in and op-out option in all of your emails. Consult a professional email newsletter provider if you decide to create this kind of publication.[49]

I hope these ideas motivate many of you to create media for your community that celebrates the values of the kingdom of God. We've got the greatest message—we need to be more aggressive in our use of the great tools of technology we have to share it. Quit complaining about the media—create it.

CHAPTER 15:

Easy Ministry Marketing Is Pervasive and Partnering

In Acts 1:8, Jesus said, "You will be my witnesses." Our witness (our marketing) is pervasive—it is everything we do, and it occurs every time we encounter another person.

All of the advice given on how to create Ministry Marketing amounts to nothing if your life and the life of your church doesn't match your words.

A strategic example: the Church Welcome Center

One of the first places visitors come in contact with your church's Marketing Ministry is the Welcome Center. Your church may have the most brilliant, seeker-friendly visitor packet ever made. It may have a kiosk that took a fortune to build. The volunteers who manage that great kiosk may wear colorful, attractive vests. But how those people who staff the Welcome Center treat visitors is most important.

> *Everything that a company does—from the way it paints its trucks to how long it takes to answer your telephones, to what the people in your factories tell their friends—communicates with the public. So everybody in the company needs to know and understand the strategy.*[50]
> —Sergio Zyman,
>   former chief marketing officer for the Coca-Cola Company

> *Preach the gospel at all times. If necessary use words.*
> —St. Francis

Your church must be proactive in this area. You can't assume anything. You must clearly define how visitors should be treated, how questions should be answered, and the attitude you expect volunteers to exhibit at all times. If you don't provide this kind of instruction, at best the church Welcome Center runs the risk of becoming a place staffed by moderately grumpy people who would rather be somewhere else. At worst, a scenario such as this following true story can happen.

A Welcome Center nightmare

Once, a single lady arrived at church. Recently divorced, her husband had left her for a woman twelve years her junior. The new wife was newly pregnant, and even though this lady had wanted children, fifteen years of marriage had not produced a child. Desperately lonely, this newly single, Christian lady wanted to go to church in a new town. She arrived before Sunday School class, thinking that in a smaller class she might have a better chance at meeting some new people. Upon arrival at the church, she visited the Welcome Center and asked about classes.

"What age are your children?" barked the Welcome Lady manning the center, who, it seemed, did not want to be interrupted.

"I...I don't have any children," the single lady mumbled.

"Well, we organize our classes around the age of your children," the Welcome Lady repeated.

"But I don't have any children," the single lady mumbled again.

The Welcome Lady laughed. "Well," she continued, "I guess there's no place for you here!"

The single lady ran sobbing to her sister who attended the church, and her sister and a friend took her to a class.

The single lady in this story had a sister to run to.[51] Not everybody does. How many other people have had similar experiences with "Welcome Ladies?" How many have received a similar response and never returned? Far too many, I fear.

Experience with Welcome Centers usually isn't welcoming

My husband and I once studied start-up churches and we visited many of them. I would always visit the Welcome Center as part of my informal research in church marketing. Though no one could top the insensitivity of the woman in the story above, my experience with Welcome Centers was, sadly, seldom pleasant. Most often the people staffing the Welcome Center were talking to fellow church members and did not want to be bothered.

Frequently, they did not know the answers to questions or have informational materials for visitors. I lost count of the number of times they were out of gifts for visitors, packets, or whatever welcoming information was intended for visitors.

Visitors with gaping wounds in their hearts come to churches every week. A spouse walked out after twenty years. A child died of an overdose. A factory closed and the pension plan evaporated. This is the life experience of so many hurting people. These are the people who dress up as best they can, try to look like everything is ok, and come to church. What do they encounter? Put yourself in a visitor's place and then be intentional about the welcome you want visitors to receive.

If you want to have lots of baby Christians born in your church, what are you doing to prepare the nursery?

Just as the attitude of the people who staff key welcoming positions sends a message, the condition of the church building also sends a Ministry Marketing message. Make it a positive message by making your church the most welcoming, pleasant place it can be. Think of your church as the nursery for potential baby Christians and make it as wonderfully welcoming as you would for an expected new baby in your family. To help do that, take a walk around the church and ask the Lord to help you see it as an unchurched person would. Here are some things to look for:

- When you get out of your car, is it clear how to get to the main worship area, the nursery, the coffee area, or the adult education classes?

- What are the bathrooms like? They must sparkle. It also helps if there are enough of them that the women don't have to form a line out the door between services.

- Is every room, facility, nursery—every part of the building and grounds—in the best condition it can be? If you have attended the same church for a long time, then you may not see the pile of half-broken chairs in the education room, the paint-chipped cribs in the nursery, or the broken fixture in the bathroom. Visitors do notice these things, and while it my not be fair, your Ministry Marketing message suffers for it if they aren't in good condition.

Two critical "S" word issues: signs and smoking

Signs

You've got to have signs. Few churches pay enough attention to directional signs, and many people go back to their cars before they attempt to find the nursery or the adult education class with no signage.

Directional signs are immensely important in churches and almost no churches have them. I teach seminars in churches all over North America and most of the time, if there isn't anyone to ask, I can't find my way to anything. Churches aren't like McDonald's or Wal-Mart—they are all different in layout. You need maps, banners, marked indications on the floor, and signs outside the doors to rooms that tell people where they are when they get there. For example, how do I know I've arrived at the "Fireside Room" if I've never been there? If I'm a few minutes late I won't know there is a fireplace at the far end of the room because I can't see through the door that is already shut.

This is a real challenge for church leaders who practically live at the church, because many become immune to seeing the need for directional signs. Pray for eyes to see what a visitor sees.

If you want to get ideas on how to improve your use of signage, go to a local hospital. Hospitals are experts in helping people find their way around because hospitals know that lives are at stake if directions are not clear. Souls are at stake for the church, so consider adding signage to your Ministry Marketing mix.

Think about putting in a smoking area

That got your attention, didn't it? This is not even possible for some churches to consider and that's okay. However, take a deep breath and hear me out.

I realize how horrible this suggestion is for many people in the church. Personally, I have a severe allergy to smoke and cannot be near it without lots of medication. But I also know many people who come to church, both the saved and the searching, who have tobacco dependencies. Attending church events that go for several hours without a cigarette is difficult for them.

I became aware of this situation recently in a small church my husband and I were helping. We were holding a Purpose-Driven Life Sunday School class that met after the worship hour and was very popular and going well. The church was actively involved with a local rescue mission and a number of men enrolled there also attended the church. But none of them came to the class. When I asked them why, one man was finally honest enough to tell me that the guys couldn't go that long without a smoke. Since that church totally forbade any smoking, either inside or anywhere on its grounds, they just stayed away.

I often hear church folks say, "We don't expect unsaved people to act like saved people." But I find that usually means, " . . . just so long as they act unsaved away from us."

When we talk about "winning the lost at any cost," we seldom consider that might mean creating a smoking area and letting people know it is okay to step out and have a smoke between church programs.

If we want to get really radical, we might go so far as to make it a pleasant place to relax and chat, like a garden or a comfortable lounge, and not just a butt can around back by the parking lot. I recently heard about a large church in L.A. that did just that. Not only did they have an extensive outreach ministry to unchurched people, but many of their praise band members were new followers of Jesus. Coming to church from the music industry, many of them were used to a smoke between performances. To love them, no matter where they were on their pilgrimage, the church built a lovely, peaceful, "Smoker's Garden." Imagine how much easier that makes it for a newly converted band member to ask a friend to come to church.

Easy Ministry Marketing Is Partnering

> *Securing volunteers in the future will be harder than in the past. The pool of those who come forward with little or no encouragement is shrinking . . . [therefore,] the responsive volunteer manager is likely to sponsor social functions for volunteers, provide experiences designed for their spiritual renewal, confer awards for years of service, and arrange a number of other benefits that will recognize their contribution.*[52]
>
> —From *Marketing for Congregations*

Ministry Marketing partners are the people who do the publications work with you, including the church staff and volunteers.

Remember, *everything* you do in the church, especially every publication, contributes to the Ministry Marketing message of your church. It is essential for the production process of ministry materials in your church to be as coordinated and intentional as possible.

It is important for you to express your care for the people creating your Ministry Marketing materials in very practical ways, and here are some ways to do that.

Give them authority

In marketing publication production, church leadership should decide on basic themes and messages, and perhaps even the overall look of publications. However, there should be a distinct handoff of responsibility at some point. When it comes to layout, final editing of articles or announcements, and the enforcement of deadlines for material submissions, allow church staff and volunteers to take the lead. Don't undercut the people responsible for the final steps of production. Stepping in as an authority when it is not necessary makes church staff and volunteers grumpy, and it shows in their work. People can tell when a grumpy person has put out a church publicity piece or weekly bulletin.

Publicly announce and print your decision

Public acknowledgement of staff and volunteer authority is a good idea. You might say something like this:

> *Jenny Smith, our communications coordinator, has final editing authority relating to layout, deadlines, and*

content of materials that go into the bulletin and newsletter, and our church's Ministry Marketing products. She has posted her guidelines and submission deadlines on the church's website. You may also find them in the newsletter and on the office bulletin board. Please support her decisions and deadlines.

Back up your decisions

Invariably, people will test the rules. When new deadlines are instituted various church members will come rushing in at the last minute with an article that just has to get into the newsletter. When the communications director tells them it is past the deadline, you know what they will do. They will walk right around that person's desk and into your office and say, "She isn't being very Christian today. She told me I missed her deadline and you need to tell her to get this article in there!"

Be sure you answer by saying, "She is being very Christian. I have given her authority over that area. She does her job in a way that honors both God and the church." Any other answer will not only make the publication creation process a mess, but it will also greatly harm your relationship with your communications director, Ministry Marketing coordinator, or volunteer.

If you are concerned about volunteers meeting publication standards, keep key church marketing and identity pieces produced in the church office under strict control. At the same time, be more flexible with the many additional pieces, such as invitation cards, postcards, flyers, and niche newsletters.

Give them training

Training for staff and volunteers is an essential step in insuring quality Ministry Marketing production by your marketing partners. Consider these consequences if you don't take the time and money for training:

Lack of training wastes valuable resources

Every dollar used in the church for computer work is a dollar that cannot be used elsewhere in ministry. Make the most of computer investments by training staff and volunteers to use equipment properly and efficiently. Money spent to make certain the staff knows how to use equipment properly is good stewardship.

Lack of training wastes people

Typically in the church, someone on staff or a key layperson who is comfortable with technology, decides that the church needs a particular computer system or software upgrade in order to create church publications. These items are purchased and then, usually without any training at all, the church secretary attempts to get the job done using these new tools. Through many tears and prayers publications are created, but the emotional and mental stress of doing it without training is seldom worth the hours wasted.

Options in hardware and software training

There are many ways to be trained. Ask people to decide what works for them. Here are some ideas:

- Some training is readily available—take time to read manuals and software help files that come with the equipment and software.

- Person-to-person training can be very helpful. You may have an expert layperson at the church who can provide it.

- Computer user groups often post training information on Internet message boards.

- Online training—training offered on the web—is expanding almost daily.

- Many community colleges offer training programs.

There are many types of training available, but one thing is certain: For most people, the computer skills required for effective Ministry Marketing are challenging and require significant time and money. Be sure to invest in training if you want to have well-equipped workers in Ministry Marketing. You can't create effective marketing without it.

Give them high speed Internet access

Broadband, high-speed Internet access is an important asset for effective Ministry Marketing. There are incredible resources available on the web, including training, free templates, clip art, articles, and more. In order to access these resources adequately and without wasting work time, provide your staff with DSL, cable, or some other method for high-speed Internet access.

Give them awards and encouragement

Honor and thank staff and volunteers in front of the church. Know them well enough to determine what kind of gift or monetary reward would be appropriate. For some people it may be a gift certificate to Starbucks. For others it may be one to a Christian bookstore.

Find out what the going rate is for graphic designers in your area. People know that church publications work will probably provide far less reimbursement than secular marketing jobs, but there is a point when the difference becomes insulting. This is especially true at a large, wealthy church that pays generous salaries to some staff members. If your communications person has become highly skilled, don't wait until he or she leaves before you realize his or her value— you may end up paying far more at that time. Do remind your Ministry Marketing staff that what they do matters for eternity, and at the same time pay them decently while they are doing their job here on earth.

CHAPTER 16:

Easy Ministry Marketing Is Properly Equipped and Prayer Saturated

This is a book about Ministry Marketing, not about the details of desktop publishing. To stay on topic and to help you produce Ministry Marketing efficiently, I won't address the multitude of production options available. Instead, I'm going recommend two pieces of equipment: Microsoft Publisher® and the RISO Digital Duplicator.[54]

> *Use the most appropriate production system your organization has—not necessarily the best.*[53]
> —Mark Beach,
> Editing Your Newsletter

In all of my seminars I take an informal survey and solicit comments on the software and hardware people use to create Ministry Marketing products. Both MS Publisher® and the RISO consistently rank the highest. They are also the tools that I use the most.

Characteristics of proper equipment recommendations for Ministry Marketing:

- They work for every size church, either alone or in conjunction with other products.

- They are inexpensive to acquire and use.

- Minimal training is required for maximum success.

- They are what I use to create Ministry Marketing projects and I couldn't do without them.

One software program: Microsoft Publisher®

The software program that you use may be different from Microsoft Publisher®, and my recommending it doesn't mean you need to totally change what you are doing. Many people use Microsoft Word® or WordPerfect® for marketing and communication projects.

Though these are great programs, they are somewhat limited when it comes to doing marketing pieces. Large churches sometimes partner with professional print shops and need to create their files using PageMaker®, Quark®, Photoshop® or InDesign®. If this is the case in your situation, keep doing what you are doing. However, for the nuts and bolts production of publications that drive the real Ministry Marketing of the church, consider using MS Publisher®. It will help you create most of your jobs much more easily than other programs.

Why MS Publisher® works for many church marketing projects

MS Publisher® is a true page layout program, not just a word processing program with page layout capabilities. This is an important distinction to understand. MS Word® and WordPerfect® work well with straight text, but when images are added, the demand for flexibility increases. Most word processing programs link words together, but graphics must be put in boxes and this makes working with complex layouts difficult. In contrast, everything in a true page layout program, including the text, the headlines, and the graphics, has its own box. These elements can then be moved, overlapped, layered, and manipulated easily.

MS Publisher® isn't a high-end, designer page layout program. This makes it much cheaper to buy (around $100 instead of $500-$800). Also, other publishing programs don't have MS Publisher's® templates. A template is ready-made design, and is the *best* thing about the program. The design is already done, the typeface is chosen, and the clip art is in place. While these elements can be easily changed, you don't have to change much to create great publications. You will probably modify the templates more as you become more familiar with the program, but in a hurry, you can always use them as is.

Publisher saves time, the scarcest resource

I am a professional designer. If given enough time, I can design about anything. However, when my pastor husband gets a great publication idea at 8:00 a.m. on Sunday morning, and it has to be created, printed and handed out by 9:30 a.m. for the Sunday School class, I don't have time to play "designer." I go to the computer, open MS Publisher®, pick a template, and *voila!* The job is done ten minutes later, and it looks great.

The templates in MS Publisher® come in families of design. That means there are templates for business cards, postcards, flyers, brochures, newsletters, and booklets that compliment each other. Use family templates to cut and paste basic information into various formats and easily produce a coordinated advertising campaign for a ministry.

It's easy for a team to use

MS Publisher® makes it easy to put together a publication team. In the previous chapter on partnering we talked about how important it is to have a team of people working on all the publications needed to fully market your ministry. With MS Publisher® you can get a site license that allows up to five individuals to use the software for a little over $100.[55] (Please contact Consistent Computer Bargains, listed in the Resource Section, or another certified reseller, to obtain a site license.) After providing your folks with training, you now have a team trained on the same software. The person in charge of publications can use or create basic templates and rely on his or her team to help with production.

I highly recommend this team approach. The only negative about MS Publisher® is that it is not available in a Mac version. However, it can be run on a Mac in Virtual PC mode. A number of my seminar participants have reported that this works well for an office that shares Macs and PCs.

One hardware recommendation: The RISO Digital Duplicator

All kinds of great ministry items can be created with MS Publisher®, but how can they be produced in the quantities needed and at a low enough cost? I have used the RISO Digital Duplicator for almost ten years and I don't know what I'd do without it. There is no other way to produce such a high volume of church Ministry Marketing materials at such an affordable cost.[56]

It's not a copier or printer; it's more like a print shop in a box

The RISO is a totally different tool than computer printers and copy machines. It is called a print shop in a box because it uses ink on paper technology similar to a printing press. Designed for jobs that require over twenty copies, the RISO isn't intended to replace copy machines, laser printers, or color printers. Each of these machines has its place in church offices. However, the RISO is perfect for high-volume printing required for postcards, newsletters, bulletins, business cards, etc.

One of RISO's most useful features is the way it handles any kind of paper stock. Because it has a straight paper feed path, paper jams are minimal. The straight paper path, combined with a completely heatless printing system, enables the RISO to print card stock, door hangers, paper bags, construction paper, newsprint, envelopes, and gummed labels, in addition to all the standard bond and stationary papers used in the church. Also, most of these can be printed super fast at 120-130 copies a minute.

The cost enables you to produce the volume you need

The cost is fantastic: a fraction of a cent per copy when printing over thirty or so copies. Because so many Ministry Marketing pieces are produced in large quantities in order for them to be effective, the RISO really is the way to go. Churches on limited budgets can now meet their marketing needs with the RISO. For example, 20,000 postcards only cost about fifty dollars. At that price you can do quite a few postcard marketing campaigns.

You can also spot-color printed pieces with a RISO, and the spot-colors don't cost any more than black ink. Use spot-color for churches and logos, and to create your own stationary, envelopes, and business cards. For just a small amount of money, you will have created a coordinated, professional-looking set of marketing pieces.

If you haven't seen a RISO, it's hard to imagine how it works; it really is different from what many folks use. Almost anyone can use the RISO, and it takes very little training to be able to run one. Because there is no heat involved, it has few mechanical problems and seldom needs repairs. Find a church in your area that has one and watch it work. That's the best way to check it out. You can find a local resource through www.riso.com. Additional contact information is in the Annotated Resources section.

Producing publications for start-up churches

Once, a pastor who worked with church plants told me that she recommended that every start-up church get a RISO, even before purchasing a copy machine or any other expensive equipment. "You can do some smaller office jobs with multi-function laser printers today," she said. "But small churches, church plants, and churches that want to increase outreach publication production should invest in a RISO. It is cost-effective and easy to use, and will produce all of the things that churches need, including stationary, bulletins, postcards, and newsletters. It really helps new churches get going."

For more ideas and examples

If you use MS Publisher® software and a RISO Digital Duplicator, the volume of Ministry Marketing materials you can create at low cost is amazing. For additional ideas on how to use MS Publisher® and the RISO visit my web site at www.cyberservants.org or www.ministrycom.com. I'm hoping to put up more actual projects by the end of this year. Regardless of what you find on the web site, talk to a friend who uses a RISO or try one for your church; that's the best way to for you to personally check out how it can help your print ministry.

Finally, no matter how well you equip your church in software or hardware, prayer is the most important tool of all, which I'll discuss in the following final section.

Easy Ministry Marketing Is Prayer Saturated

> God will do nothing except in answer to prayer[57]
>
> —John Wesley

This book hasn't just been about marketing—it's about Ministry Marketing. Though there are some overall principles that apply no matter what kind of marketing you do, there is an additional reality that is important to acknowledge as we end our discussion on Ministry Marketing. That reality is the power of prayer—before, during, after all of your projects.

This book has been about telling our story well and illustrating the power of prayer in Ministry Marketing, so let me end with three stories.

A church bulletin found at McDonald's shows kindness

In response to my comments on the importance of church bulletins, a pastor shared this story with me at one of my seminars:

> At my church there is a man who has been coming for a number of years. He's really grown in the faith and is very active in the church. Not long ago, he said, "Pastor, I've never told you how I came to come to the church have I?"

> "No," I said, and he proceeded to tell me his story.

> "I'd just gotten out of prison. I was really discouraged and feeling very suicidal. I didn't have much money, so I went to McDonald's to eat. As I was sitting there, I saw some sort of publication on the floor. Not having anything better to do, I picked it up to read it.

> "It was the bulletin from the church. I read through it and I decided to come to the church. I came because, from reading your bulletin, you looked like a church who would be kind to me."

Trash found under a bush leads to a new life

During a seminar break, a church secretary shared this story:

> Most of the time we never know how our materials affect people, but the Lord let me know about one such time.

> Like you recommend, I always think it's important to put a gospel presentation in as many publications as we can. You never know who might read it. I did that even though people thought it was silly of me.

> The publication that I do is a synod newsletter for Lutheran church secretaries. People told me everybody who would read it was already a Christian and effort to present the gospel

every time the newsletter is published was a waste of space. I still felt it was important.

A few months ago I was visiting a pastor to get his news and he told me about a young lady who had recently come into his office. Apparently she was the crossing guard at a public elementary school near the church. One day, as she was waiting for her shift to start, she noticed the wind had blown some trash beneath a bush where she was standing.

Being a tidy person, she reached down to pick it up. It was my newsletter. She had some time before the start of her shift, so she read it. She had grown up in a totally secular family and when she got to the gospel presentation, it was the first time she had ever heard that she could have a personal relationship with God. She wanted to know more.

As soon as her shift was over she noticed that one of the churches listed in the newsletter was just a block away. She went there, burst into the pastor's office, and said, "Tell me about this!"

After a series of several conversations the pastor led her to a personal relationship with Jesus. But that isn't the end of the story. A few months went by, and at the end of the quarter I was back at the church to get the news for the newsletter.

"Remember that young lady that became a Christian from reading your newsletter?" the pastor asked me.

"Yes!" I replied. "How is she doing?"

"Well," he said sadly, "I did her funeral this morning. Her death occurred very quickly. Not long after she became a Christian, she wasn't feeling well and she went to the doctor. After a biopsy, the doctors found that she was just filled with cancer inside. There wasn't anything they could do. She died peacefully last week."

This woman and I were both a bit teary as she ended her story, but then she said to me, "It's just good to hear about the effect of the work we do."

That desktop publishing stuff really works!

The lady standing in front of me almost yelled these words to me as I was eating my sandwich during one of my seminar lunch breaks.

> "It really sounds like you mean it," I replied, "Tell me your story."

> "I do!" she said. "Here's why: years ago I didn't go to church, didn't care about God or any of that. Then I got a divorce. I don't know how this church got my name and address but they did. They started sending me all this stuff about their single's group.

> "I'd get it and throw it in the trash. I thought it was dumb. Stupid and dumb. This went on for months and I kept throwing their stuff in the trash.

> "But one night, I was really lonely. So I dug a postcard out of the trash and went down to the church.

> "To make a long story short, I started attending the church. I got saved. I met my current husband there."

She told me she was currently the director of a Christian camp. As we continued to talk, she said she never found out who sent her those postcards.

There is always a balance

This book has been filled with many stories, ideas, suggestions, reminders, and commands. If you attempt a fraction of the ideas you've read, you'll be busy for a long time. Let John Wesley's advice inspire your Ministry Marketing:

Do all the good you can,
By all the means you can,
In all the ways you can,
In all the places you can,
At all the times you can,
To all the people you can,
As long as ever you can.

Do all of that. Work as hard as you can. Apply the advice and ideas from this book and from all the other resources I have recommended. Repeat your marketing projects and get them out to your targeted audience over and over again. Having done all that, don't forget to pray. The following are some specific suggestions for prayer.

Practical prayers for Ministry Marketing

- Pray for wisdom as you create your materials. There are always many possible approaches, all of which might work. Our Lord knows the hearts and exact needs of the people you are trying to reach. Ask for wisdom and insight as you decide the approach to take.

- Pray for understanding and skill in using your tools. Every job goes easier if your tools are a help and not a hindrance. This prayer may involve a prayer for time and money for training.

- Pray for peace in the church office and protection from distractions. Chaos, discord, arguments, and misunderstandings can affect the outcome of your Ministry Marketing in negative ways. Pray for protection from that and that your office and publications reflect the peace and joy of Jesus.

- Pray for perseverance and wisdom in repetition of your message and a smile and happy answer to self-appointed critics.

- Pray for receptivity on the part of your audience when they receive your Ministry Marketing materials. Pray they don't get lost in the mail or e-mail; pray people are in a good mood and don't ignore them; pray they post them on the refrigerator, tell their friends and attend.

- Pray that you will tell the gospel story well so that many will respond to it. Pray they will begin a personal walk with Jesus and your church community, and ultimately become part of the story that C.S. Lewis describes as:

  ...the Great Story, which no one on earth has read: which goes on for ever; in which every chapter is better than the one before.[58]

SECTION FIVE:

Resources

An Invitation

No one book can contain all of the insights, tips, advice, and conclusions that thirty years of Ministry Marketing has taught me. One thought that comforts me is my belief that each book, essay, or article we create becomes part of a continuing dialog between author and audience. For those who have taken my seminars or read previous books and articles, consider this part of our conversation. For new readers, I hope this has been a useful introduction.

Help me continue to tell the story. Please let me know your response to the book. Send me your ideas, resources, suggestions, and questions. E-mail me at yvonprehn@aol.com. I cannot promise a personal response, but all e-mails will be read.

Annotated Resources

The resources below have been useful to me in my Marketing Ministry, and I will share with you why I've included a resource in this list. The web address information is current as of this book's publication. However, know that web addresses frequently change.

Many other resources are listed in the body and endnotes of the book, and I tried not to repeat them. This list is far from exhaustive. There are many wonderful resources that perhaps I have not discovered. Please e-mail me and let me know your favorites and suggestions. My e-mail address is yvonprehn@aol.com.

Yvon Prehn's Web Site

http://www.ministrycom.com or http://www.cyberservants.org

This site a is useful resource for Christian Marketers and Communicators. You will also find seminar schedules for my seminars, held all over the U.S. and Canada, and lots of free articles, tips, and resources.

Evangelism, Outreach, and Postmodern Culture

Covell, Jim, Karen Covell, and Victoria Michaels Rogers. *How to Talk About Jesus Without Freaking Out: An Easy to Use Practical Guide to Relationship Witnessing*. Sisters, Ore.: Multnomah, 2000.

Detweiler, Craig and Barry Taylor. *A Matrix of Meanings: Finding God in Pop Culture*. Grand Rapids: Baker Academic, 2003.

To paraphrase a psalm—the pop culture today declares the glory of God, if only you've got eyes to see it. This summarizes the message of this book. All around us in movies, sports, advertising, and television are messages and dialogs about the eternal. Tuning into these images will enable us to dialog with a world that needs to be introduced to the Word made flesh in Jesus. This is an important book for any church leader who wants to reach out. The book provides a good understanding of the postmodern mentality and approach to life, without getting hung up on the word itself.

Kamp, John. *Out of Their Faces and Into Their Shoes: How to Understand Spiritually Lost People and Give Them Directions to God*. Nashville: Broadman & Holman, 1995.

McLaren, Brian D. *More Ready Than You Realize: Evangelism as Dance in the Postmodern Matrix*. Grand Rapids: Zondervan, 2002.

Miller, Donald. *Blue Like Jazz: Nonreligious Thoughts on Christian Spirituality*. Nashville: Thomas Nelson, 2003.

This is not a book about postmodern. It is a postmodern native speaking. I loved this book. I almost couldn't quit crying at his description of walking up to a campfire where Jesus is sitting, of being able to see the lines on his face and of talking to him.

Mittelberg, Mark. *Building a Contagious Church: Revolutionizing the Way We View and Do Evangelism*. With contributions by Bill Hybels. Grand Rapids: Zondervan Publishing House, 2000.

Strobel, Lee. *Inside the Mind of Unchurched Harry & Mary: How to Reach Friends and Family Who Avoid God and the Church*. Grand Rapids: Zondervan Publishing House, 1993.

Sweet, Leonard. *Carpe Manana: Is Your Church Ready to Seize Tomorrow?* Grand Rapids: Zondervan, 2001.

———. *Post-Modern Pilgrims: First Century Passion for the 21st Century World.* Nashville: Broadman & Holdman, 2000.

———. *Soul Salsa: 17 Surprising Steps for Godly Living in the 21st Century.* Grand Rapids: Zondervan, 2002.

———. *SoulTsunami: Sink or Swim in New Millennium Culture.* Grand Rapids: Zondervan, 1999.

Read any book by Leonard Sweet. He was talking postmodern, living it, experimenting with, commenting on and celebrating postmodern, when most us were still saying, "Huh?"

Apologetics

Sometimes people are afraid to market their ministry and share their faith because they aren't sure of it themselves. Take time to become sure. These resources can help.

Strobel, Lee. *The Case for Christ.* Grand Rapids: Zondervan Publishing House, 1993.

———. *The Case for Easter.* Grand Rapids: Zondervan Publishing House, 2004.

———. *The Case for Faith.* Grand Rapids: Zondervan Publishing House, 2000.

Lee Strobel's books are some of the best books on the truth and trustworthiness of the Christian faith that I've ever read. Read everything this man writes, memorize it, and you'll gain confidence and assurance.

Equip: The Online Ministry of Christian Research Institute, http://www.equip.org.

This is the web site of the Bible Answer Man and on it you can get all sorts of great Christian apologetics resources, articles, position papers, and copies of the many excellent books by Hank Hanegraff.

Christianity Explored, http://www.christianityexplored.com.

Contains a new evangelism study from England. The study uses examples and illustrations from current media and sports and is honest in its presentation of the cost of becoming a Christian and the consequences of ignoring Christ. The site also has a wonderful book to give people who don't know Jesus.

Pop Culture

Hollywood Jesus by David Bruce, http://www.hollywoodjesus.com.

This is a fantastic, crazy, and wonderful web site about Christian interpretations of movies, TV, and other media. This is a great resource if you want to use movies and media for outreach or if you want to learn to watch them and learn it's possible to see them as parables and bridges to our culture. The creator, David Bruce, is a wild, modern, fearless marketer for the gospel. Study his methods—he touches souls today.

Church Growth Resources, Conferences, and Web Sites

While there are many, many other approaches and resources in other denominations and churches, these are the ones I have learned the most from and currently use in ministry. Go to any and all of these resources to fill your ministry marketing toolkit.

Southerland, Dan. *Transitioning: Leading Your Church through Change.* Grand Rapids: Zondervan, 2000.

This book is about so much more than its subtitle implies. It is an excellent book on how things happen in churches when we look at marketing as everything that goes on. Southerland's advice on segmenting your market is excellent.

Warren, Rick. *Purpose-Driven Church: Growth without Compromising Your Message and Mission.* Grand Rapids: Zondervan, 1995.

This is a classic and it gives helpful and practical church marketing insights.

―――. *The Purpose-Driven Life: What on Earth am I Here For?* Grand Rapids: Zondervan, 2002.

Ginghamsburg Church, http://www.ginghamsburg.org.

Ginghamsburg Church's web site doesn't have the sort of massive material as previously mentioned sites, but what is available is very valuable for Ministry Marketing. The site highlights the ministry of Mike Slaughter and his extraordinary church. These folks were early pioneers of multimedia products and they are still among the best.

Saddleback Church, http://www.saddleback.com.

This web site is for Saddleback Church. You'll envy and drool and want to move to Southern California (probably not). If not, you'll definitely find lots of great church ideas.

Purpose-Driven Church Ministries, http://www.purposedriven.com.

This is the web site for the Purpose-Driven Church ministries, conferences, and resource materials. You may also call them at (949) 609-8700.

Sermon Transcripts, Outlines, and Audio Resources by Rick Warren, http://www.pastors.com.

Willow Creek Church, http://www.willowcreek.com.

This is the web site for the many resources available from the Willow Creek Church, materials by Bill Hybels, and others associated with him. You may call them at 1-800-570-981.

Christian Web Sites

American Tract Society, http://www.ATStracts.org.

Tracts are a fantastic outreach and marketing tool for your church! If you haven't checked out ATS's selection of gospel tracts, call them as soon as possible. Their phone number is 1-800-54-TRACT. ATS's selection is fantastic. Every year I read through the Bible using their Bible reading schedule, which guides you through the Bible in the historical order that the events happened.

Barna Research Online, http://www.barna.org.

George Barna's organization runs this web site. The Barna organization conducts all sorts of studies and provides statistics on a variety of developments in the church and society. Sign up for the free e-mail newsletter at the site. It will give you summaries of his latest studies.

Bible Gateway.com: a Ministry of Gospel Communications, http://www.biblegateway.com.

I love this site! You can look up any Bible verse and just cut and paste it into your word processor. Lots of translations are available.

Gospelcom.net: a Ministry of Gospel Communications, http://www.gospelcom.net.

This is a comprehensive Christian web site. Hundreds of Christian ministries useful to Ministry Marketing are linked to this site. Youth Specialities, the American Tract Society, and many others will give you ideas on how to do effective Ministry Marketing.

Marketing

Direct Marketing Association, http://www.the-dma.org.

This is a huge site for professional, direct mail, and other marketers. It is expensive to join, but there are lots of articles, resources, and ideas for non-members.

North American Mission Board, http://www.namb.net/ads.

> *Part of the Southern Baptist Church media resources. NAMB provides radio and TV clips that can be customized. It is also a good place to look for marketing approaches and information for start-up churches.*

Printing and Publication

BlanksUSA: Genuine Blanks, Diecuts, Perfs, and Scores for Copiers, http://www.blanksusa.com.

> *This is a wonderful source for all sorts of blank paper products, including door hangers, postcards, envelopes, table tents, or almost everything you can imagine to run through a RISO or laser printer.*

Printed training materials

Dummies books, http://www.dummies.com.

> *"Dummies" resources are classics for computer students, but you can't go wrong using them and having them on hand for your church staff.*

Smart Computing Magazine, http://www.smartcomputing.com.

> *They have an online magazine you can subscribe to and lots of resources for learning about and answering questions on computer technology.*

Christian Technology

Bill McKenna's site, http://www.wwsg.com

> *If you have a RISO and are not getting the quality of photos from it you would like, Bill McKenna has a CD called,* Scanning and Processing Photographs for the RISO. *The CD costs $49 and has helped lots of folks.*

Christian Computing Magazine: Applying Tomorrow's Technology to Today's Ministry, http://www.ccmag.com.

> Christian Computing Magazine *has been around for a long time and is still the most useful source available for information about Christian computing. The editor, Steve Hewett, is a true pioneer and visionary in ministry computing, electronic communications, and marketing. If you want to know what's coming and how to prepare your church, Steve will talk about it in the magazine and at his national annual conferences. CCMag now has a new online version that may be the future of publications—be sure to check it out. One other benefit: Yvon Prehn writes articles on desktop publishing and communications each month.*

RISO, http://www.riso.com.

RISO's web site offers information about this great "printing press in a box" for churches and a place to sign up for their free Expressions newsletter.

Technologies for Worship Ministries Magazine, http://www.tfwm.com.

These folks publish a magazine, hold conferences, and have a web site that is one of the very best sources for multimedia, music, drama, high-end PowerPoint® production, and all kinds of contemporary worship elements. This can be an important part of your marketing mix and you can learn so much from this group. Their web site is an incredible resource because you can go back for years, search for topics and download the articles for free. The yearly conference has very high-end resources and training is available.

Site Licenses and Software

Consistent Computer Bargains, http://www.ccbministries.com.

All sorts of software at fantastic prices for churches and nonprofit ministries are available from Consistent Computer Bargains. Their prices for site licenses for Microsoft products (useful in a church office setting) are unbelievably low. This is where I recommend you get MS Publisher® to outfit your communications team. They are wonderful people and very helpful.

Volunteer Recognition

Energize: Especially for leaders of volunteers, http://www.energizeinc.com.

A fantastic site that also provides a very good free email newsletter. Lots of information, articles, books, resources and link give you ideas on working with volunteers.

Harrison Promotions, Inc., http://www.harrisonpromotions.com.

Harrison has a VIP line (Volunteers are important people) with aprons, mugs, lapel pins, etc.

Voluncheer.com: Celebrating Good Works, Remarkable People, http://www.voluncheer.com.

Volunteer has all sorts of cute things, from cookie cutters to candles to recognize volunteers—great gifts for the bulletin stuffers!

Notes

1. Mouw, Dr. Richard, quoted in the Los Angeles Times Magazine.

2. Barna Research Online, *Beliefs: Salvation*, http://www.barna.org/cgi-bin/PageCategory.asp?CategoryID=4.

3. As a potential Ministry Marketer, be sure you learn your message well. See "Apologetics" in the Annotated Resources section for sources that will give you the knowledge and encouragement you need.

4. The church program itself doesn't matter nearly as much as what you do with it. Pick one and work it.

5. Todd Kappelman, "Marshall McLuhan: 'The Medium is the Message'" *Probe Ministries Intl.*, (2001), http://www.probe.org/docs/mcluhan.html.

6. Steve Hewett, editor, *Christian Computing Magazine*.

7. Philip Kotler, *Marketing for NonProfit Organizations* (Upper Saddle River, N.J.: Prentice Hall, 1975), 9.

8. Charles H. Spurgeon, *Morning and Evening* (New Kensington, Pa.: Whitaker House, 2001).

9. Alexander Hiam, *Marketing For Dummies* (New York: Hungry Minds Inc., 1997), 1, 3, 20.

10. Ibid., 1.

11. See the Annotated Resources section for more information about these teaching churches.

12. Donald Miller, *Blue Like Jazz: Nonreligious Thoughts on Christian Spirituality* (Nashville: Thomas Nelson, 2003), 238-239.

13. George Barna, *Church Marketing: Breaking the Ground for Ministry* (Ventura, CA: Regal Books, 1992), 140.

14. *"Americans Speak: Enron, WorldCom and Others Are Result of Inadequate Moral Training By Families,"* Barna Research Online, July 22, 2002, http://www.barna.org/cgi-bin/PagePressRelease.asp?PressReleaseID=117&Reference=D.

15. Martin Peer, "Buddy, Can You Spare Some Time?" *Wall Street Journal*, sec. B1, January 26, 2004.

16. Dale McFeatters, "What Workers Do with Their 'Free' Hours," *Ventura Star Free Press*, February 2, 2002.

17. Craig Detweiler, and Barry Taylor, *a matrix of meaning, Finding God in Pop Culture* (Grand Rapids: Baker Academic, 2003), introduction, 84.

18. Lyle Schaller, *The Very Large Church* (Nashville: Abingdon Press, 2000).

19. Mark Mittelberg, *Building a Contagious Church: Revolutionizing the Way We View and Do Evangelism* (Grand Rapids: Zondervan, 2000).

20. Ibid., 59

21. Barna Research Online, *Beliefs: Salvation*, http://www.barna.org/cgi-bin/PageCategory.asp?CategoryID=4.

22. Barna Research Online, *Comments on Easter*, http://www.barna.org.

23. Sarah Pike, *"New Age and Neopagan Religions in America,"* Columbia University Press, http://www.columbia.edu/cu/cup/catalog/data/023112/0231124023.htm.

24. C. S. Lewis, *"Myth Became Fact,"* cited in *The C. S. Lewis Encyclopedia,* ed., Colin Duriez (Wheaton, Ill.: Crossway, 2000), 138.

25. Leonard Sweet, *Soul Salsa: 17 Surprising Steps for Godly Living in the 21st Century* (Grand Rapids: Zondervan, 2002), 12.

26. Brian D. McLaren, *More Ready than You Realize* (Grand Rapids: Zondervan, 2002), 9.

27. Ibid., 84, 85.

28. Dan Southerland, *Transitioning: Leading Your Church through Change* (Grand Rapids: Zondervan, 2000), 59.

29. Ronnie Lipton, *Designing Across Cultures* (Cincinnati: HOW Design Books, 2002), 10.

30. Ibid.

31. Ibid., 122, 123.

32. Ibid., 10.

33. Ibid., 11.

34. Jay Conrad Levinson, *Guerilla Marketing* (Boston: Houghton Mifflin, 1984), 76.

35. Detweiler, *a matrix of meaning*, 26.

36. Ibid., 11.

37. Tice, Rico and Barry Cooper, *Christianity Explored* (Cumbria, UK: Authentic Media, 2003), 4.

38. www.puravida.com This is an incredible group that provides great coffee and any imaginable coffee service your church might need and the proceeds go to help at-risk children in coffee-growing countries. You can purchase your coffee from them and sell the coffee to raise money. Set up a latte stand; they will help you do it.

39. C.S. Lewis, *God in the Dock: Essays on Theology,* ed. Walter Hooper (London: Collins, 1979), 8.

40. Susan K. Jones, *Creative Strategy in Direct Marketing* (Lincolnwood, Ill.: NTC Business Books, 1998), 5.

41. Sometimes money is not a determining factor for a church's postcard marketing projects. Church size, quality expectations, and finances are all determining factors. If a church has enough money, there are wonderful resources available that can effectively and professionally take care of these concerns. See Chapter 14: Easy Ministry Marketing Is Programmed and Publicity Proactive for a list of these resources.

42. Mittelberg, *Building a Contagious Church: Revolutionizing the Way We View and Do Evangelism,*

43. Levinson, *Guerilla Marketing*, 21.

44. Mark Beach, *Editing Your Newsletter*, Cincinnati: Writer's Digest Books, 1995), 6.

45. Norman Sahwchuck and others, *Marketing for Congregations* (Nashville: Abingdon Press, 1992), 216.

46. Doorhanger note and blanks recommendation, go to www.blanksusa.com.

47. PhoneTree, http://www.phonetree.com.

48. Hiam, *Marketing for Dummies*, 185.

49. See the web site Constant Contact by Roving, http://www.constantcontact.com.

50. Sergio Zyman with Armin Brott, *The End of Advertising As We Know It* (Hoboken, N.J.: John Wiley & Sons, 2002) 41.

51. There is a happy ending to this story. Fastforward six years from this event. The lady in the story is now married to a pastor. They began a single adult ministry at the same church. It eventually involved more than 300 singles and was the largest, most active, singles ministry in Ventura County, California. One of the slogans for the ministry was, "There is a Place For YOU here!" I know the story well; it's my story.

52. Norman Sahwchuck, *Marketing for Congregations.*

53. Beach, *Editing Your Newsletter,* 17.

54. For additional discussion, instructions, resources, and ideas on production software and equipment, visit my web site at www.ministrycom.com. [correct url] For an excellent guide to other tools that can be used for the creation of multimedia ministry marketing materials, see Tim Easom's book *Ministry Marketing Made Easy* (Nashville: Abingdon Press, 2003).

55. Please contact Consistent Computer Bargain for detailed information. See the Annotated Resources section.

56. For more information, go to http://www.RISO.com.

57. C.S. Lewis, *The Last Battle* (Collier Books: New York, 1956), 184.